THE DAY I WAS

O L D E R

❧

ON THE POETRY OF

DONALD HALL

THE DAY I WAS
OLDER

ॐ

ON THE POETRY OF

DONALD HALL

EDITED BY LIAM RECTOR

THANKS TO THE GENEROUS SUPPORT
of the
NICHOLAS ROERICH MUSEUM, NEW YORK

ISBN: 0-934257-20-5 (cloth)
ISBN: 0-934257-19-1 (paper)

Book design by Lysa McDowell
Story Line Press
403 Continental Street
Santa Cruz, California 95060

Library of Congress Cataloging-in-Publication Data

The Day I Was Older: On the Poetry of Donald Hall/
edited by Liam Rector.
    p.   cm.
  Bibliography: p.
    1. Hall, Donald, 1928–   —Criticism and interpretation.
I. Rector, Liam, 1949–
PS3515.A3152Z65 1989
811'.54—dc19   89–4403
                                   CIP

CONTENTS

AN INTERVIEW WITH DONALD HALL

COMMENTARY II

REVIEWS

PHOTOGRAPHS OF DONALD HALL

INTRODUCTION

The occasion for this book is the mounting achievement of Donald Hall's poetry, an achievement presaged by an early precosity and sometimes overshadowed by Hall's deserved eminence as a person of letters. There have been many reviews of Hall's work over the years, a sampling of which is included here, but very little sustained, intelligent criticism. This book then looks to begin to redress that situation, and yet it is not a book of scholarship or critical commentary upon an entire *oeuvre*, per se. Many of those I invited to contribute original essays are long-time colleagues and admirers of Hall's work, and I trusted their merry contention to not turn the book into uncritical homage, a testimonial timepiece offered up to the altar of a recent retiree. Donald Hall is anything but retired.

Hall's poetry reached an apotheosis with the publication of *The One Day* in 1988, months before Hall's sixtieth birthday, and the response to that masterwork is only touched upon in this book, published shortly thereafter. We are therefore commenting here essentially *en route*, and this is primarily a book of memoir, a book of attention to both the work and the life of a poet whose contributions have existed in many dimensions but must be finally appreciated and judged by what has been at the center of that vortex—the work of his poetry. There are few who have so deeply embodied the literary history of their times to the extent that Donald Hall has, both in the body of his poems and in his work as editor, *provocateur*, essayist, anthologist, prose stylist, dramatist, biographer, polemicist, publicist, teacher, and general ramrod on behalf of literature.

Hall has believed in and brought home for us all a sense of work (what in New Hampshire is called *wuk*) and his example has been a great tonic to the solipcism and granite careerism which forms too often the unambitious and ungenerous milieu in which we find ourselves. Sometimes when the old dogs get too mellow you have to give them a kick in their ribs to get them barking again. Donald Hall has never stopped barking.

The One Day brings us to that signature book wherein the entirety of a poet's former materials are orchestrated and melded into a single presence whereby one can no longer tell the dancer from the dance, so united is the step and the movement between steps. Building upon a lyrical power we might also associate with Yeats (whose work has haunted Hall's from the onset), and complicating that myth-building with a montage form both reminiscent of and an advance upon a latter-day Modernism, the achievement of *The One Day* is made all the more rare since the book-length poem in three parts is a cacophony of multiple protagonists, built using lyricism as but an article of the conjure. It is a doing of what is now conscious but was before unconscious in our language, an enacting of the many voices in both our individuated consciousness and our *polis*. It's been said that Donald Hall found his "voice" most mightily as a poet first in his book of poems of 1978, *Kicking the Leaves*, and I think there's *some* truth to that. As you'll see from the brief selection of poems included here, culled from years of his work, he had already found parts of that colony of voice. (Voice is understood here to be not the confessing or monologuing "self" of the author—I doubt there is such a thing as any single self—but the "I is an other" wherein character itself is burned through, burnished into the work of art itself.) To invert Yeats, I think with *Kicking the Leaves* and with *The Happy Man* in 1986 Hall began to find not only the *image* but the *book* of his poetry. With *Kicking the Leaves* Hall began to write his one poem in its "onlyness"; with *The Happy Man* he extended the world of *Kicking the Leaves* and simultaneously discovered the direction that was to find its culmination, again *en route*, in the restless and poignantly ranting repose of *The One Day*.

The progress of Hall's work, as with most real progress, has been one of fits and starts, presumption colliding with experiment, blind alleys gone down and exhausted, triumphs hard won and accidentally gathered, and whole tendencies of time and the times lived out — written through. There is an insistent adolescent equation in American thinking (should it be called American *attitudes?*) which I think goes something like this: what is old is bad and what is young is good. It is at once part of our infantile stupidity and our naive exuberance. The word *old* is something of a key to Hall's work and thinking as he has, as much as any American poet ever has, looked to find what is good, worthwhile, enduring about what is old, what is perhaps even redeeming within the fist fight, glory, contradictions, delusions, and the love which constitute our often troubling personal and tribal histories. What has saved him from being a mere archeologist or dour historicist is that as a poet he has also incessantly been hell-hounded artistically by the battle cry of one of his greatest teachers, hearing constantly Ezra Pound's taunting, "Make it new." As an only child Hall grew up in a world of grown-ups, oldsters, and the particular roadster he's travelled down the American highway has been to perversely become more young as he keeps his bloody eye on aging.

My own engagement with Hall's work and presence began

in the late 1960s in America, a time which opened out just as my own adolescence was opening out, just as I came upon two anthologies of poems which then offered up a dialectic, a contrary for their time — *New Poems of England and America*, edited by Hall, Robert Pack, and Louis Simpson, in 1957, and *The New American Poetry*, edited by Donald Allen and published in 1960. I suspect it's difficult for any sixteen-year-old now, as I was then, to imagine how any anthology or two anthologies of contemporary poetry could have such import, such priority, such *command* on anyone's attention — given that our recent anthologies are little more than collation devices, almost cynical packagings (from whatever aesthetic) which have no editorial nerve whatsoever — but those two anthologies were both presentiments of an aesthetic cleavage and quarrel that would haunt for a good while the immediate post-World War II generation of poets, poets now in or approaching their sixties in age. Whether it was academic versus beat, cooked versus raw, or the deeper argument of what Hall has called constructivist versus expressionist, those bodies of work, as disparate and desperate as each contributor's work was, opened out an abyss which is still in some senses the work of my primarily revisionary generation to fill — this in addition to the poetry of the past and the Woody Allen apocalypso of our own tragi-comedy. We've had Hall and Ginsberg to inherit, the equal formalism of Bishop and Creeley to answer to, and the great Modernist grandparents who still, in a "logic of classical consummations," form our immediate and, I think, our closest ancestry.

Now that the dust has in some ways cleared, it's obvious that the poetics of both anthologies emanated basically from the Pound ear, the Pound era, even if one essentially took the tack of T.S. Eliot and the other William Carlos Williams. What I now hear most in Hall's work is the motive, ambition, and range of Pound, wrought in a more succinct manner. His recent work has brought us full circle, back from revision to vision, from "ecumenicism" to full power regained for an expressionist and constructivist vatic voice, an encompassing sweep which provides a horizon for our current moment, the mad scientist laboratory of our editing rooms. So much "material" has been shot—so many images, so much blood on the cutting room floor. . . . Hall has in his poetry and his commentary chastened the "McPoem" in us and restored what is truly ours to inherit, imagine, and move on with. If Allen Ginsberg's "Howl" and "Kaddish" are likewise landmark achievements in our poetry, as they certainly are, in the extended poem of The One Day I hear Donald Hall's "Moloch" being the essential idleness of our late civilization, revising our greed as the last thirty years have revised our innocence about it.

For the old fan of Hall's work this book will then be a book of appreciation, an accounting for the long road travelled thus far. To the new reader, I hope it will provide some introduction. I trust it will send both readers back to the poems themselves, forward to their own ambition and what they might earn of it.

Liam Rector
Virginia, 1988

COMMENTARY I

DONALD HALL AND THE TIGER

❧ Robert Bly ❧

I'm going to concentrate here on *The Happy Man*, more particularly on the long poem called "Shrubs Burnt Away," with sideways looks at other poems. In *The Happy Man* and his 1978 book called *Kicking the Leaves* Donald Hall is doing his most substantive work. Literarily, he has created a lively short line and a lively long line. He has overcome a tendency toward mechanical rhythm that his long line exhibited in the 60s and 70s. His short line, as apparent in the poem called "Whip-poor-will," is now positively elegant in its use of sound, and its pitch variations remind us of some of the best poems of William Carlos Williams.

One could also mention a spiritual advance. First of all, he works in *The Happy Man* to create an eye that can see granite as a form of grass; and he pulls heavy objects sometimes into the world of transparency and spirit. Several poems express the soul's longing to know other worlds.

> Here love builds
> its mortal house, where today's wind carries
> a double scent of heaven and cut hay.

Finally, in this book, he is able—for example in the poem "The Baseball Players"—to see moments of eternity clearly in the midst of muddled daily life.

Psychologically, the book is complicated. The psychology

in his early books tends to be clear—too clear, with naked oppositions of country and city, conscious and unconscious, repression and expression which take place against a mess of lies hinted at in the background. Now he brings the messy background to the foreground.

He wrote in earlier books as a critic of his father's side of the family. The men on his father's side worked mainly as businessmen in the last two generations; on his mother's side there were farmers and, among both men and women, schoolteachers. Donald Hall's father gave up a possible career as a prep school teacher in order to work in his own father's dairy in Hamden, Connecticut. All his life he chided himself, Donald Hall says, for not doing *what he wanted to do*. When Donald as a boy visited the New Hampshire farm owned by the mother's side of his family, he experienced the traditional life of the farmer, and preferred that to the life in Hamden. Comparing the two ways, he criticized his father's way, and beyond that, all suburban life, and beyond that, the entire middle class. He praised in his poems and prose what he had learned to love in New Hampshire: the slow pace of farm life, the alternation of seasons, the ritual of haying, the care for cattle and other animals, the extended families, the relatedness. This life he described beautifully in *String Too Short to Be Saved*, a prose book which is still a masterpiece of recollection.

During the years he attacked the middle class most sharply, he made his living as a university professor. Such a vocation proved to be, in view of his psychology, a hard place in which to stand. It entangled him in self-shaming on the one hand, and an uneasy nostalgia for a vanished life on the other.

He brought the two sides closer together by moving into the old New Hampshire farmhouse in 1975, establishing his life with

Jane Kenyon, each of them doing what they do. He is not a farmer; he doesn't farm the land, but he does live firmly on it.

Whether a person does what he or she wants to do becomes a prominent theme in "Shrubs Burnt Away," and we will turn to that poem now. The speakers in the poem do not have names, so one needs to read carefully to find out who is who. The lives evoked do not correspond in any detail to the lives of Donald Hall's father and mother, grandmother, etc., so the poem is not strictly autobiographical. The poem is *composed* and we have a right then to consider the chosen details important and intentional.

The main speaker is middle-aged, a drinker, a smoker, nostalgic, fond of his yellow chair, adulterous in the past, now Calvinist around sexuality, full of memories of his childhood, aware of betrayals he has himself done. He has a mother who he mentions sang songs to him when he was a child, and he refers briefly to his father, who worked in a lumberyard. We'll call him Horace, just for fun.

The second main speaker, who is a woman, has a great number of stories to tell. Her words are set in quotation marks so we can easily identify her talk. She is not related to the first speaker, and apparently the two have never even met each other. She loved drawing and painting when she was a young girl; then for a long time did not do "what she wanted to do." In later age she has become an active and well-known sculptor. We'll call her Henrietta, just to have a name for her.

Henrietta tells several stories about her own parents. Her mother was alcoholic, hooked on pills, and an adulteress as well. Henrietta as a child was looking for a playmate named Bingo.

"We were chasing each other and ran into a clearing
And found Bingo and Harold's father and my mother
Drunk, rolling on the grass with their clothes off."

Henrietta's father, cuckolded in this way, throws a drink
into her mother's face, and then drives at high speeds down
the dark roads. Apparently some time later he dies in a
car crash.

Henrietta's reminiscences include some scenes that appear
to be drawn from Donald Hall's childhood memories. The imagined family that lives the life which the poet has been so idealistic
about shows a dark and murky history when investigated. That
fact means to me that we don't have a simple contrast
anymore — a bad suburb versus a good farm. The writer brings
in daydreams and night dreams; and the people living on the
"good farm" have disturbing dreams. Horace tells one dream
of a sexual party, and Henrietta describes two dreams, one of
a plane crash and one of the execution of children. Horace
daydreams about floods carrying away houses, of middle-class
homes being burnt down, and so on. Both of the speakers appear
to have been let down by the older generation in some way.
Both have experienced early failures that seem to reflect long-
standing family neuroses. Horace says:

I lay in the dark hearing trees scrape
like Hauptmann's ladder on the gray clapboard.
Downstairs the radio diminished, Bing Crosby,
and I heard voices like logs burning, flames
rising and falling, one high and steady, one
urgent and quick. If I cried, if I called . . . I called
softly, sore in the wrapped dark, but there was nothing,
I was nothing, the light's line at the closed door faint.
I called again; I heard her steps: —
Light swept in like a broom from the opening door

and my head lay warm on her shoulder, and her breath
sang in my ear — A Long Long Trail A-winding,
Backward Turn Backward O Time in Your Flight . . .
In the next room a drawer banged shut. When my father
lay dying at fifty-one, he could not deliver
the graduation speech at Putnam Avenue School
near the house he was born in. Taking my father's
place, my head shook like a plucked wire.
I told the fourteen-year-olds:
Never do anything except what you want to do. . . .

Once a little boy and his sister — my mother lay
on top of the quilt, narrow and tense, whispering —
found boards piled up, deep in the woods, and nails,
and built a house for themselves, and nobody knew
that they built their house each day in the woods . . .
I listened and fell asleep, like a baby full of milk,
and carried their house into sleep where I built it
board by board all night, each night
from the beginning; from the pile of boards I built it,
painted it, put doorknobs on it . . .

The line following "Backward Turn Backward O Time in Your
Flight" is "Make me a child again just for tonight."

Is there any doubt but that a longing for union with the
mother underlies many of these lines and hovers around the
stories of grownups told elsewhere in the poem? We have a situation that the Freudians called the fundamental situation: longing
for early union with the mother, hostility toward the father —
sometimes conveyed by condescension — and attraction to tales
of sexual activity seen by children. The question being asked
is: "Where does the sexual libido — unused — in the child go?"
Freudians traditionally fail to imagine any mythological place
where this libido could go — for example, toward "The Heavenly
Pair," to the Imagined Woman, to Aphrodite. This failure of

imagination traps the child in its constantly disappointed state. The woman to whom all these incestuous longings go — the personal mother — cannot produce the remembered Eden and so disappoints the child. Everyone is disappointed. The psyche as a result is not a good container: desire energy leaks out in constant fantasy toward the personal mother, and the psyche then as a result cannot maintain its firm desire to achieve an artist's life. The inability to "do what you want to do" is precisely the speaker's charge against his own father and Henrietta's charge against herself and against her mother.

There is much helplessness and victimization in the stories: children abandoned in the crib by the mother, mistreated, forced to see what they don't want to see. It's as if their lives were eaten up by older people. Henrietta recalls:

> "The year after my father burned in the wrecked car,
> my mother came home early from the job she hated
> teaching bookkeeping at the secretarial college.
> Sometimes she wept because she had flunked someone
> she had caught cheating. Each day I comforted her;
> I was fifteen years old. I cooked supper for her —
> hamburgers and hot dogs, baked beans, corn niblets.
> Once I took a recipe from *Confidential Chat*,
> using asparagus soup, Ritz crackers, and water chestnuts.
> She said I would make some man happy."

The mood is psychic despair, depression, passivity. Neither the main speaker nor Henrietta are doing what they want to do and the older generation seems to have failed at that too. The main speaker as a boy was playing the games of grown-ups, for example, milking and calling calves. We don't see the boy playing the games of children his own age. Nostalgia may be associated with having grown-up playmates when young. We

know from other poems that Donald Hall on the farm as a boy
played the grown-up games with the grown-ups, but they are
dead. Does that mean that when he plays he must play with
the dead people? Well, that is the way it is.

Horace tells one of his dreams:

> There was the dream of the party: a French farce,
> frolic behind curtains, exits and entrances—
> like a child fooling parents. I departed
> alone on a bus that bumped down the white staircase
> of the mansion over the bodies of three women
> who stood complacent and pretty in the bus's way,
> their faces familiar as photographs. When I looked
> back from the bus's rear window at their bodies,
> they waved to me although they were dead:—
> They forgave me because no one was driving the bus.

The dream hints at some sort of depreciation of Eros. A bus
rolls over three women; they wave and they forgive the dreamer
"because no one was driving the bus."

Henrietta dreamt this scene:

> "I wait for the plane inside a blockhouse
> at the airport's edge; then the cement walls vibrate
> as if an earthquake shook them. I understand at once:
> The plane from Ireland has crashed trying to land.
> Immediately I watch a conveyor belt
> remove bodies covered with brown army blankets
> from the broken snake of the fuselage. One of the dead
> sits up abruptly, points a finger at me,
> and stares accusingly. It is an old man with an erection;
> then I notice that all of the dead are men."

This dream might imply that the young male Eros has crashed
or died—that is "the plane from Ireland"—while the only Eros
left is associated with old men.

All through the poem we notice a loss of energy through alcohol and aimlessness. Mythologically I sense some sort of being or figure who eats the forward energy particularly of the men. Toward the end of "Shrubs Burnt Away," one last dream of Henrietta is recounted; in it an ominous figure appears. It is a beekeeper or a person with a beekeeper's masked face. This figure supervises the cutting up of the children.

> "I am sad in the convenient white kitchen, dreaming
> that I weep as I start making dinner.
> The children themselves weep, bringing their sentences
> on small folded squares of blue paper.
> They will take pills to die without disturbance.
> I help them count the pills out, and arrange
> pillows for their comfort as they become sleepy.
> While I slice onions and peppers on the breadboard,
> someone whose identity hovers just out of sight, the way
> a beekeeper's mask darkens a face,

> "walks up the busy street and enters the kitchen
> to instruct me in butchering the children.
> The visitor picks up the long rag doll and with scissors
> carefully cuts the doll's limbs at the joints,
> teaching me expertly, with anatomical explanations
> and a scientific vocabulary, while cutting and preparing
> the model, then places the doll's parts
> on a high shelf, arranged with the gaps of
>   dismemberment
> visible, so that I may consult it while cutting,
> as I must do, as it seems that I want to do."

The poem as a whole lays out a description, even a narrative, of the sort of life that activates the beekeeper. I would say that this figure has moved in to grow enormous at the expense of the passive or the undifferentiated male soul. What can Henrietta or the main speaker do when they feel themselves threatened by this beekeeper? Elsewhere in the book the writer offers an option — living a boring conventional life unobserved. The poem is called "Mr. Wakeville on Interstate 90":

> "Now I will abandon the route of my life
> as my shadowy wives abandon me, taking my children.
> I will stop somewhere. I will park in a summer street
> where the days tick like metal in the stillness.
> I will rent the room over Bert's Modern Barbershop
> where the TO LET sign leans in the plateglass window;
> or I will buy the brown BUNGALOW FOR SALE.

> "I will work forty hours a week clerking at the paintstore.
> On Fridays I will cash my paycheck at Six Rivers Bank
> and stop at Harvey's Market and talk with Harvey.
> Walking on Maple Street I will speak to everyone.
> At basketball games I will cheer for my neighbors' sons.
> I will watch my neighbors' daughters grow up, marry,
> raise children. The joints of my fingers will stiffen.

> "There will be no room inside me for other places.
> I will attend funerals regularly and weddings.
> I will chat with the mailman when he comes on Saturdays.
> I will shake my head when I hear of the florist
> who drops dead in the greenhouse over a flat of pansies;
> I spoke with her only yesterday . . .
> When lawyer elopes with babysitter I will shake my head.

> "When Harvey's boy enlists in the Navy
> I will wave goodbye at the Trailways Depot with the others.
> I will vote Democratic; I will vote Republican.
> I will applaud the valedictorian at graduation
> and wish her well as she goes away to the university
> and weep as she goes away. I will live in a steady joy;
> I will exult in the ecstasy of my concealment."

Only tremendous fear could force a man to contemplate such a boring life. If he lives so, apparently he will escape the beekeeper's notice; or alternately, he will already have

diminished himself so much that there is no more to diminish.
What else do we deserve? We were conceived by the rabble left
behind when the aristocrats went to Ceylon.

> While Lady Ann grew pale playing the piano, and lay
>   late in bed aging,
> she regretted Rathwell who ran off to Ceylon with his
>   indescribable
> desires, and vanished—leaving her to the servants who
>   poached, larked,
> drank up the cellar, emigrated without notice, copulated,
>   conceived, and begot us.
>
>   (from *The Revolution*)

We can say that Horace in the long poem is very hard on
himself. His critical "I" is overactive, sees no redeeming feature
in the reckless living of sexual impulse, and sees no redeeming
feature even in old love affairs.

> The world is a bed, I announce; my love agrees.
> A hundred or a thousand times our eyes encounter;
> each time the clothes slough off, anatomies
> of slippery flesh connect again
> on the world's bed, and the crescent of nerves
> describes itself again in the wretched
> generality of bliss. If we are each the same
> on the world's bed, if we are each manikins of the other
> then the multitude is one and one is the multitude;
> many and one we perform procedures of comfort.

In several poems, the speaker longs to die—by car crash, or
rifle. The beekeeper encourages the interior critic. I feel considerable art in this introduction of the beekeeper. Most people
understand the beekeeper very well, and know how much
damage he has caused their lives. He judges life, cuts it up, puts
its possibilities to sleep, acts like the judge at any unfair trial.

Of course we have no right to say that the beekeeper is "he." The author carefully avoids pronouns. The poem about the old woman in the rocker who observes male suicides with equanimity suggests that the beekeeper may be female. Whether male or female in tone, the beekeeper assists in the cutting up on the dolls and the severing of life from its desire-ground. I think we have to thank Donald Hall for going into this serious brooding as deeply as he has. He may be afraid, but he continues to work anyway.

I am not saying that Donald Hall intended to lay out these last observations about the beekeeper or the Old Lady in the Rocker who eats libido, particularly, it seems to me, libido when it has lost its goal, but that is what the poems say. I think that with his image of the beekeeper he has added an important contemporary detail to the ancient pictures of the Devourer, that is the Great Mother in her eating mood or the Great Father in his eating mood. The courage of the writer lies in his repeating: something or someone has eaten up my family, or more accurately, has eaten up the desire–energy of the two families being described. That is enough to say in one poem.

Understanding that expressed fear helps us to set an otherwise puzzling epigraph into place. If we imagine the Devourer as a tiger, we can understand the paragraph from Hsu Hsia–K'o: "Mi–t'o Temple after Thirty li. A most desolate spot . . . For fear of them hiding tigers, all trees and shrubs have been burnt." The book's epigraph from Tolstoy goes:

> Behold me then, a man happy and in good health,
> hiding the rope in order not to hang myself to the
> rafters of the room where every night I went to
> sleep alone; behold me no longer shooting, lest
> I should yield to the too easy temptation . . .

SOMETHING HARD TO GET RID OF:
AN INTERVIEW WITH ROBERT BLY

Marty Lammon

MARTY LAMMON: Doing this interview with you reminds me of Hall's story in *Remembering Poets*. Hall went to interview T.S. Eliot and brought with him two "technicians" — Louis Simpson and yourself.

ROBERT BLY: Yes. The days before I had said: "Don, let me go with you." He said, "No, Robert." "Come on Don. He'll be dead before so long. I'll never get to see him if you don't take me along." "No, Robert. You never behave yourself, you'll say something wrong." Louis was with us and he said, "Come on, Don, take me along too, come on, it's not fair." Don said, "No, I'm not taking either one of you along. Robert never behaves himself, and I'm going by myself." We really complained, we cussed him out. But something fell through. The next day he came by and said, "Robert, may I use your tape recorder?" "Aha! Both Louis and me . . ." "All right, all right, I'll take you both along; you and Louis will be tape recorder technicians; I'll introduce you both as tape recorder technicians." So, that's the way it happened. We were glad to go!

LAMMON: That's excellent. You and Hall first met each other at Harvard, didn't you? How did you meet and what experiences do you recall?

BLY: Oh, I remember it very well! I was a Sophomore when I got there and Don was a Freshman. And I had joined the *Harvard Advocate* a few months before — I'd suppose I'd been an editor for a couple months or so. He tried out as a Freshman — yes, I think that's right. I remember I met him in the *Advocate* office. And we talked, that night; our attitudes were very different . . . but then we agreed to meet the next day, and we started consulting about poems, and we've been close friends ever since.

LAMMON: You were involved with the *Advocate*, then, as an editor?

BLY: There was one main Literary Editor — I had that job in my Junior year. . . Don would have been a Sophomore that year. The year I was a Senior. Don became the Literary Editor. I remember that very well. The *Advocate* was always in financial trouble. To help I put out a special issue "For the Sixtieth Birthday of T.S. Eliot." It was a special issue . . . sixtieth birthday! But I didn't proofread the title page very well, and it announced the occasion as his *sixteenth* birthday. For the issue I reprinted some early poems of Eliot's from the *Advocate*, at the time he was an editor. They were very interesting little poems, some influence of Laforgue visible. Eliot a few months later wrote a letter to the *Advocate* and he said, "I recently had a great surprise upon opening a copy of the *Harvard Advocate* to see reprinted poems of mine that I wrote when I was an undergraduate, and I must say that if I had wished to have these poems reprinted, I would have done so myself." He was right. We all said, "This is terrible. Now we've turned him against the *Advocate!*" Don Hall said, "It's all right. I'll write and tell him that the previous editor did it, and he's gone now!" And I said sure, go ahead. So he did. Later, Don went to see him when on his way to Oxford, and that's how his friendship with Eliot began. It began with my stupidity!

LAMMON: Earlier, you mentioned in our conversation today that you thought one of Hall's best books was *String Too Short to Be Saved*. I agree.

BLY: Yes, it will be a classic of American Literature in fifty years or so.

LAMMON: You talk of that book as being a classic in fifty years or so. Who do you think — of the poets writing today — will last? Whose poetry will be read from generation to generation . . . fifty years from now? Donald Hall?

BLY: I think so. Well you know Frost . . . Frost has a very interesting view. Some poets . . . I remember during the Viet Nam war, people would say to me, if you mention the Viet Nam war in your poem, that poem will not be universal because the war will pass. So there's this talk about universal poetry. I don't accept that view at all. Frost had a different view. He said that what you hope to do is to write a couple poems that are hard to get rid of. That's a very different idea . . . Obviously, if they're hard to get rid of, it must be because they have something in them that hooks people, hooks onto their clothes. Such a poem has to have some of the dark side in it, otherwise it wouldn't hook you. "Stopping by Woods on a Snowy Evening," that everyone loves, makes clear that Frost had to fight against a strong desire to lie down in the snowy woods and die. The poem contains that admission; the admission is done in a very elegant and sidelong way. But we all have or have had that desire, so the poem hooks into our dark side.

LAMMON: Would you say that Donald Hall is writing any poems which hook into that dark side?

BLY: Yes, I would. He has written, like all of us, many poems that do not do that. We have all written descriptive poems, or family poems, or childhood poems — you work your way through something . . . all such poems are *necessary*. You have to write a lot. But I know "The Long River" is one that's going to be very hard to get rid of. And it's possible that the "Pig" poem may be hard to get rid of . . . it's called "Eating the Pig." I thought that when I read it the first time. The center of it comes down into eating. There's something frightening about eating. Don takes an interest in eating, and suddenly he's eating the land between the Tigris and Euphrates Rivers . . .

LAMMON: But then, also, there's a sense of not just eating those places, but also being consumed yourself. I think Donald Hall has a tremendous preoccupation with the whole dying process . . .

BLY: You're right. I know poems of his in which the whole process is described as a cycle; and it's symbolized in the cycle of water — the idea first appears in that poem about falling snow ["The Snow," from *A Roof of Tiger Lilies*] — and now it appears in different forms. Did you see the little children's book he did? It's about a year old. It's about an old farmer. The old man owns an ox and he makes a wagon . . . then he fills the wagon with what he has grown and objects he has made. He drives the ox and wagon to upstate New Hampshire; then he sells in the market place all the things he has grown or made, then he sells the wagon, then he sells the harness; finally he sells the ox. Then he walks all the way home; and the night he gets home, he starts to make a wagon again. It is a cycle, and children understand that. It's one of the most brilliant children's books in fifteen years. The illustrations are brilliant too. People have raved about it, and I think that is partly because the poem—it is a poem—contains a cycle. You make things with your own hands, and later, completely stripped, walk all the way home and start it over again. He has a new poem in which the cycle appears in chicken-raising: it begins with the baby chicks arriving in the mail—he does a lot of work with sound in this poem, so that the chirping is *heard*. The poem then follows the growth of the chickens, the pullets become layers, then after a few months the laying falls off and they are ready to be sent off for killing—and it ends with him and his grandfather and grandmother sitting down to eat a chicken dinner. The issue comes up, who eats *them?* Again he follows the cycle all the way around in an ordinary situation, not the extraordinary or romantic mood of snow and rain, but in a domestic, human situation—one sits down, and eats chicken, at the table—and there's some mysterious question asked. Is there someone eating you? So strong!

LAMMON: You mentioned sound a bit ago. So much of Hall's work stresses rhythm and sound and line. Sound and rhythm seem important to your work but subordinate to the image. Would you say there's a divergence between you and Hall?

BLY: Yes. So far. I have been trying to teach him something about the image for a long time. Not the concept, but what it can do. And he has been trying to teach me the importance of sound for years. About a year ago, I began to compose a few poems in which I pay careful attention to the sound—the sound really dominates the poem. And he recognized that and saw that his ideas had finally reached me. He was amazed! We have things we try to teach each other. Lately, he's been attacking my syntax — he's after my syntax — and I'm learning a lot from him. I have a habit, which I took from Whitman probably, of using overly simple syntax. The other day I sent a prose poem to Don — a first draft. It is a kind of thing poem. I describe a group of ten roses, and then slowly begin taking associative steps outward or downward from them. Each step I take is a phase, with its own image. Don said: "Robert, have you ever heard of any other grammatical marks besides the comma?" He's trying to make me understand that there's got to be more to syntax than laying down phrase after phrase separated only by a comma.

LAMMON: Hall talks about a concept called "the vatic voice" which, as I understand it, deals with the unconscious imagination, some knowledge inside us that is released during moments of intense energy. This idea seems to grow directly out of your poetry and your idea of image. Would you comment on Hall's phrase "the vatic voice"?

BLY: Well, that is odd, because in a workshop this afternoon a woman asked: "What's your definition of a poet?" I said, "Why do you ask?" she said, "Well, my boyfriend says that a poet is someone who prophesies." She was describing a Vates. The Romans said that there are two kinds of poets; one is the ordinary poet of feelings and the other one is the Vates through whom tremendous psychic material passes. He or she allows himself or herself to be a channel for it. Don Hall believes that this distinction is important. In Rome, Virgil was the only vatic poet. Of course, he was the one Dante chose. And the "poets of feeling" are not inferior poets at all, but different — perhaps they choose the material, but the Vates is a channel. Both have to shape it once it has come. I'm not sure what the relation of the image is to that. I'd guess that the vatic poet goes deeper into the unconscious than the other poets, and to some extent he is carried there by the image. The image helps human beings to get to the unconscious. I *also* believe that *music* helps human beings to move toward the unconscious.

LAMMON: You're using the dulcimer, trying to bring music back to your poetry?

BLY: Yes, I like music with poetry. Vatic poetry probably makes more use of silences, too, than ordinary poetry, because the unconscious material has to have time to sink in.

LAMMON: I think my next question relates to this idea of "the vatic voice." Poets, good poets, operate on many different levels. We've talked about levels of unconsciousness the last two days. Could you examine Hall's poetry and perhaps discuss what levels he's trying to operate on?

BLY: Well, we'll have to find a single poem to talk about, but since we've mentioned "The Long River," let's take that one:

THE LONG RIVER

The musk-ox smells
in his long head
my boat coming. When
I feel him there,
intent, heavy,

the oars make wings
in the white night,
and deep woods are close
on either side
where trees darken.

> I rowed past towns
> in their black sleep
> to come here. I rowed
> by northern grass
> and cold mountains.
>
> The musk-ox moves
> when the boat stops,
> in hard thickets. Now
> the wood is dark
> with old pleasures.

On one level it's a narrative, about a boat going down a long river, going past the sleepy town. That's the story level. On the second level it's a sexual poem, it is about love-making and the orgasm of the man. I was quite surprised to find that out, actually. I hadn't seen it. I don't think Don would mind my mentioning that. Had you seen it that way?

LAMMON: I never had.

BLY: No. I was very surprised. And I examined it, and he's right — it's there. Those "old pleasures" — the slow approach . . . very beautifully done. There is also a third level in which there is a movement from the conscious level down toward very ancient, archaic levels of the brain. It's a brain poem. I suppose you call that level a biological level, and the mind during the poem moves back towards the instinctual. To return to the second level for a moment, the sexual, that level refers to an actual *act* that the person is taking or living through, an *event*. On the third level there are no events. The poem represents the mind returning to archaic levels, for which the musk-ox and the long river are perfectly good symbols. And the fact is that the rhythm begins to slow down toward the end. His sound work in this poem is tremendous. Without that careful sound work, with "ud" and "oh," the rhythm would not slow down, and he wouldn't have been able to say what he had to say about the archaic and instinctual brain.

LAMMON: This seems to tie in with your idea of the reptilian brain and the mammalian brain.

BLY: Yes, that's possible. The musk-ox would represent what McLean calls the *mammal brain*. The mammal brain contains warmth, community, sexual pleasure: "old pleasures." A poem of his that's good is really good because he composes it with tremendous care. He rarely makes a poem in the way I composed some of the *Snowy Fields* poems, in ten or twenty seconds. He works with tremendous care and slowly one thing comes and then another thing comes.

LAMMON: All the things you've talked about relate to journey—a narrative is a journey, the river itself, going from the conscious mind to the instinctual mind is a journey. The idea of the journey seems very important to your work and to Hall's. Not just the physical journey, but also the spiritual journey. Do you think the idea of the journey is peculiar to your work and to Hall's, or is it a necessary element in all poetry?

BLY: I think it's a necessary element in all vertical poetry. We'll just make up two terms, horizontal and vertical poetry. Most poetry is horizontal poetry. Marxist poetry is horizontal, most political poetry. Most confessional poetry, I suppose, is horizontal because it blames social conditions. "Daddy" is blamed for Sylvia Plath's unhappiness. Longfellow is horizontal, most of Whittier, "John Brown's Body," e.e. cummings. Our poetry in the United States was horizontal as long as one could leave Virginia and go West and find a new place to live.

James Wright has a great poem called "Stages of a Journey Westward" — The man in it starts West, by stages, and I think he ends up as an alcoholic on the shore of the Pacific pitching whiskey bottles into the ocean. There's the most tremendous sense in that poem of the horizontal journey coming to an end. Once a nation's population flows out to its natural boundaries, once it has gone as far as it can in the horizontal direction, then it has no choice: it has to go down. At that point the poet who understands that becomes involved in journey, because the journey in poetry does not involve stages of a journey westward, but stages of a journey downward. One of the first models for that downward journey is the descent of Inanna, which was just rendered in full for the first time. (*INANNA, Queen of Heaven and Earth* by Diane Wolkstein and Samuel Noah Kramer. Harper & Row, 1981.) Inanna descends into the underworld; that has come to us in the trivialized or horizontal form with Salome's dance of the seven veils, but in the original version Inanna gives up one set of clothes at each door. God knows what that means; no one is sure. But that's what it felt like in Mesopotamia when they reached their physical boundaries. So vertical poems descend into the underworld. "The Long River" does that. I wrote about certain stages descending in "Sleepers Joining Hands." With Don the movement seems more like a circle or cycle: the descent and then the ascent and then the descent and then the ascent. I don't see many other poets dealing with this material — among contemporary poets that is. Robert Duncan does it, and sometimes David Ignatow as well.

LAMMON: Perhaps Galway Kinnell?

BLY: Yes, yes that's right. He does.

LAMMON: Talking about journeys, the descent not only into the underworld, but also the descent into the past seems important to Hall—not only his immediate past, but also the archetypal past which is inherent in all human beings. In "Eating the Pig," we talked about his eating the land between the Tigris and Euphrates, but he's also being eaten. As in his early poem, "My Son, My Executioner," there's a sense that his son eats him.

BLY: Yes, these two poems must be related. And probably another in which Don *eats* maple syrup his grandfather had stored more than twenty-five years earlier. He has always brooded more over the past, especially his family's past, than I have.

LAMMON: His family is so important to him, especially obvious in *String Too Short to Be Saved*—and in *Kicking the Leaves* he definitely returns to the themes in *String*—

BLY: He has returned to live on his grandfather's farm now, the same farm where he spent his summers as a boy. A few years ago, when I first visited him there, I wrote a poem about that experience. I was touched by the old 1865 photograph reproduced on the cover of *Kicking the Leaves*. The house and grounds have hardly changed at all!

LAMMON: Is that the actual farmhouse where Hall's grandparents lived?

BLY: That's the house. Even the trees seem to be the same.

LAMMON: Which poem is it that you refer to?

BLY: It is a prose poem that I haven't printed, and I'm not sure that I will. I've sent it to Don in a couple of drafts, and I'm not sure if it's a poem, or just a descriptive piece. And he says, "Well, I like the subject, so I'm likely to say it's a poem." It talks a little about that photograph and his grandfather and the loneliness of those woods. Jane [Kenyon] and Don and I started reading some poems together in that old farmhouse and suddenly I felt we were back 10,000 years in the past. The piece ends with that sensation. I know there's something in it, but it's also private in a way; I don't know if it will come around and be a poem or not.

LAMMON: You and Hall, then, stay very close. You mentioned earlier that you have two letters in your suitcase now.

BLY: Yes. We have a rule that when we send poems the other one has to answer the letter in 48 hours. So he says, "I'm sending you poems and I'm invoking the 48 hour rule." Then I have to answer in 48 hours.

LAMMON: You've done so much work in translating. I don't see Hall becoming involved with that kind of work.

BLY: No, he was teaching all the time. You can't do everything.

LAMMON: True. You do have a tremendous interest in East Asian studies, the Spanish poets, and poetry of other cultures — and so many other poets seem headed in that direction — whereas Hall seems very much in the English tradition. Do you think this shift in interest reflects some unavoidable trend away from English-based traditions?

BLY: I don't know. To some extent, I feel some attentive poets are being thrown off base by my studies.

LAMMON: Really? Thrown off as in disregarding — not understanding — you?

BLY: No, they're being thrown off their own center. I have always felt that, since we are Americans, it is dangerous to restrict our horizons to the English horizons. On the other hand, my influence can be bad for younger poets if it shifts them too fast into some other culture, in which they may be even farther away from their own center than they would be in English studies.

I live in the center of the country—I live very near where I was born. So there's some way in which I'm unmistakably American, and at home; I go and visit other cultures, and feel all right about it. But there may be people who really don't feel American, and moreover they may live at one or the other of the two coasts. Perhaps they feel torn away from their original background somehow, and I could be very dangerous to people like that. I think I have been. It's hard to know what is useful. To some extent the praise of foreign poetries is wonderful; to some extent, however, and for certain men and women, it means that not only won't they understand Spanish Literature, but they will lose the grasp they have or could have had on English Literature.

LAMMON: So the different cultures work together as opposed to being separate?

BLY: Yes. What happens to me is that I'm more and more interested in *Beowulf*, more and more interested in *Sir Gawain and the Green Knight*. What I have learned through Kabir helps me understand the wild stuff that's going on in *Gawain*, and what I have learned in Lorca helps me to understand the wild stuff that's going on in *Gawain*, and what I have learned in Lorca helps me to understand the wild images that appear in *Beowulf*. Actually my past lies in *Beowulf*, not only because it's in the English language, but also—from another point of

view—because it's a Viking, a Scandinavian poem. So we all
sense that the point of study somehow is to curve back to your
own tradition and see it more intensely. I'm a bad influence
if people get excited about Spanish poetry and as a result never
read English Literature. I've done them a disservice. All I've
done is increased the excitement in their minds. Don is very
stubborn—he holds firmly to his roots which lie in English
Literature, and to his farm and that area up in New Hampshire. That stubbornness may be worth more to him in the end
than all the flexibility that the surrealist poets or the New York
poets have. When things are well-rooted they are harder to get
rid of.

LAMMON: Yes. Hall has the comment—speaking of Frost,
Eliot, and Pound—that endurance is just as important as other
qualities. He says that in *Remembering Poets*, which brings me
to my last question. Have you read *Remembering Poets*, and what
did you think of it?

BLY: I thought and still think it is marvelous. It was the first
book of literary criticism my oldest daughter read—high school
age then—and she told me she's read it three or four times and
loves it. I'll say two things about it. It is superbly honest, first
of all. He met Eliot, Pound, and Thomas while he was still very
young—perhaps nineteen to twenty years old. He doesn't write
the book from later wisdom. He takes you back to his psyche
as it was at twenty or so, and he preserves his confusions and
his ignorance. That takes courage, and we realize what it was
like to meet three geniuses much older than he was. He constructs something clean and honest, no decorating, no refur-
bishing, no adding of insight. Making the book is like making
a Shaker chair, simply and cleanly. That was a good thing to

do. Unusual. I'll tell you another generous thing he did. He resisted the temptation to make the book broad or all-encompassing. He could have done that easily, by including experiences other people have had with Eliot, Pound, and Thomas. It would have been easy to say: "This incident I've just recounted reminds me as well of the outrageous thing Dylan Thomas did when he visited Mrs. Biddle . . . . " But he didn't do that, and he didn't refer to other people's interpretations of the poems. If a writer does that, the network of the book widens, pretty soon it catches all sorts of fish, events that happened to others are interpreted, images from later poems are interpreted—it's all very impressive, and the writer comes off as supremely intelligent and well-read. The problem is that one-fourth of the book is first-hand material and the other three-fourths is second-hand material. Hall has a superb critical mind, and obviously that route was a strong temptation in this book, but he didn't give in to the temptation. He wrote only of what he had experienced. He had learned that discipline writing poems, and he kept it in this book. There is something immensely intelligent, generous, and disciplined about him, and many of the gifts he has given are not yet recognized as gifts.

A HAPPY MAN

Robert Creeley

Two summers ago a copy of *The Happy Man* arrived unexpectedly and I put it aside for a bit, characteristically, just that summers seem now the only time at all open to impulsive decisions and, finally of far more value, the chance to think of things sans a distracting need to. But the title was certainly inviting — if only as contest — and Tolstoy's macabrely confident observation with respect to his own "happy" despair, quoted for the book's motto, was even more provocative.

As I read, I recognized the divers personal landscapes, the "Parker House Rolls," "Wrong-Way Corrigan," "this .22 Mossberg carbine" (I had had one), and so forth quite literally into a shifting, reflective place of summary lives, testaments of wry and articulate "personal" history, making a case, so to speak, as emphatic as styles and rhetoric of gravestones or those flatly loquacious people that Masters found in the Greek Anthology. But these folks were far closer to home, my own.

Bill Katz, an old New York friend, told me of seeing once on Spring Street, I think it was, a stone out front of a mason's shop, that is, the usual grave memorial marker, except that instead of its having decorative swirls, or nothing at all, it said simply, "Your Name Here." One needs no emphasis upon the fact that we do all lead, sooner or later, common lives, and so come to nemesis in company no matter how much we may resent it. It's a small life at best and very little proves untoward despite its initial strangeness.

One would know from a crucial earlier book of Donald Hall's, *String Too Short to Be Saved*, just how specifying and resonant his detailing can be. That work (1961) was a return to the complex place that, twenty-five years later, echoes with such effect in this collection, in the persons but even more significantly in the pattern of their speech. So, reading it, I was very moved because the stories were so dense, old time compelling, and familiar. Despite the often bleak facts — as if Robinson's people had come back to tell us more — the poems provided a curious and unexpected reassurance as one read them. I thought of my grandmother's familiar stories of violent confrontation or despair — there was some relation she'd had to Lizzie Borden, and Flaming Sarah Ware was, I think, a cousin. Much as my grandfather's narratives of his years at sea as a young man, my grandmother's told me of a human world of intensive, emblematic events, relations, for which there was neither answer nor repair. There was an extraordinary moment in an interview Truman Capote had with Bobby Beausoleil, of Manson's company, some years ago, when, questioning him about the two and a half days it took Beausoleil to finally kill the L.A. couple, Beausoleil's answer and defense was, simply, *it happened.*

Why then the pleasure? Robert Duncan notes the crucial role of the storyteller who is there, literally, to take one through the places of most terrifying kind, permitting the witness and the curious pleasure of that relief. What is it they say? The worst is over? Hardly.

In any case, I wrote to him to say how much the poems had moved me, and called the book "a beauty," which it certainly was. (If one needs a measure, think of the grotesque management of Frost's "The Witch of Coös": "It left the cellar forty years ago / And carried itself like a pile of dishes / Up one flight from the cellar to the kitchen," etc., etc. It is very hard to tell a story in this mode, the more so if the frame is a monologue, which determines the permitted context even more adamantly.) He answered promptly, "To have *you* call this book a "beauty" absolutely dazzles me. Thank you so much! I think I was about as surprised by these old-time monologues as you are . . . ." It was a very happy outcome.

Our beginnings had been very much otherwise, as though we had been committed to opposing armies with very little prospect of an "ancient inn" where we might meet and resolve our difficulties. He came to Harvard a couple of years after I had, in time to reopen the *Advocate* at the University's request after myself and cronies had caused it to be closed because of our carryings on. I recall our wary first meeting in Gordon Cairnie's Grolier Bookshop—he introduced us—but nothing at that time could really make a common ground. Then, living in France in the early fifties, I came upon a piece he had in a magazine called *The World Review*, "American Poets Since the War." He qualified the various schools of American poetry of that time, and then noted what he felt was the effectual *cul de sac* of W.C. Williams' influence and example, remarking that only Charles Olson and myself seemed still persuaded of his use. Ah well! Paradoxically, it was an immensely reassuring fact to be called a follower of anyone, since I felt entirely boxed out as a writer and with no regard whatsoever. That this generous article included me so specifically (and aptly, as it proved) was of very real use. I wrote an answer immediately, in my best rhetorical manner, and had it duly published in whatever issue was next after the December 1952 one in which his had been. So it was I engaged the literary world, and in England at that.

But years went by before we got any closer, sadly enough. Then, in the early sixties, with time free of teaching and having just come back from a makeshift tour in England, I was doing ten readings for the Michigan State Arts Council, en route home to New Mexico, back to back, the reward being that if you could stay on your feet and in your right mind, you got $1000 at the end of it all. Don's was an absolutely unexpected and delightful respite — or put more as felt and as it was, he got me together again, by speaking a language I could get with, recognizing where I was at, and knowing my own terms and commitments. It was a singularly generous accommodation.

It is, of course, that ability so to know others that informs the poems of *The Happy Man* in particular, but also goes back and back to a unique diversity of responsibilities and functions. For example, he was a crucial teacher at Michigan for the writer Tom Clark and I note Tom's relation to the present work on page 79 of that book. That matters.

When he quit teaching, I remember feeling both envious and apprehensive. It's so often the case that American poets don't easily move into the vacancy of that Big Time, the full fact of the professional literary world. More often they do what I've done, teach, or manage some comparable means of support from landscape gardening to usual business. Again it's Tom Clark I think of as holding together the daily situation, as Don, of the writer, getting what work there is, getting it written, keeping an integrity against very obvious odds. He was well taught.

One wants to say, then, what begins, or seems to, as a brightly able life, hospitably eager and willing to believe in and listen to its elders (the interviews of Eliot and Pound as the book including them, *Remembering Poets*, are singularly alert to the persons), all that cares and has cared in this man, paid attention, to details, to friends — or all that was, and wanted, to get out of it also, like a drink, or just to break the pattern, change it, remember when it was happy, and go there, which he did to his eternal credit. Upstairs, there's the attic with the studs still showing, the stuff collected, the echoes of the others previous, outside the density of the trees on the knoll, and across the way the pond, the weather. . . "Once a little boy and his sister. . . ."

THE IMMUTABILITY OF THE QUICK-CHANGE ARTIST: DONALD HALL

❦ W. D. Snodgrass ❧

In a country that chooses its leaders, intellectual or political, as we do, it's only to be expected that genuine thinkers or statesmen (if such there be) get swept into corners lest excellence mortify the many. This does, however, subject an artist to a giddying barrage of ironies and disparities — disparities of public acclaim as opposed to actual excellence, of popular image as opposed to personal character, of conspicuous change and promiscuity as opposed to surreptitious constancy and integrity. Donald Hall, more than any writer I know, has both benefitted and suffered from those contradictions. Indeed, with him, the ironies accrue nearly to sarcasms.

When he was young, Donald Hall was not, I then thought, a very good poet. Nonetheless, he was *the* arbiter of poetic taste here; his appraisal, more than anyone's, determined your place in the literary world. Now that he's made himself into one of the best poets we've had, no one pays much attention to his opinions. Except for old friends and several dozen younger writers who send him work for criticism. And scornful as he is — secure in his Harvard background — of writing programs, he has long maintained a workshop for poets and critics, a school assured of excellence by the quality of its staff. The energy he donates to others' work is all the more remarkable since he lives mostly by freelance writing and public readings; his time is doubly precious.

For many years, we knew each other only through correspondence. I believe he first accepted some of my poems for *The Paris Review*, then a second batch for *New Poets of England and America*. That anthology, which he edited with Louis Simpson and Bob Pack, first brought my work some notice. Much later, I learned that he'd known my work even earlier: while a graduate student at Stanford, he'd seen the poems in my application for a fellowship under Yvor Winters. I had thought the loss of that fellowship (not to mention the brutality of Winters' rejection letter — which, of course, I *have* mentioned) a staggering defeat; it was, in fact, a windfall. Not only did I escape further damage under Winters; I gained a friend whose critical acuity, generosity and warmth have grown unfaltering for 30 or 35 years.

Don took those poems when my affairs were at their sorriest: I had lost my first university job; I had a family to support; only publications would make me hireable, yet scarcely anyone would touch me. Once that anthology came out, things started to fall my way — publications, awards, readings, job offers. Oddly, this created a new problem: I owed any recognition I had to Don's liking my poems; I did not like his.

Perhaps this should make no difference when his later work has so far surpassed anything of that time. Still, I can't help wondering why I disliked those poems so much. My attitude would have surprised most poetry readers — they linked us in what they probably called an "academic" school. Re-reading the poems now, my disapproval seems exaggerated even to me. I may have judged him more harshly just because our work actually shared some characteristics — competition is always more fierce inside, than it is between, species. Or perhaps, in an ally, all differences seemed disloyalties.

I still do find some of the imagery and rhetoric of those poems less than convincing. Besides, a contrariety of musical preference has been lifelong for us. Nowadays, Don sends me drafts of much of his work; I send him drafts of *everything*. I do not always obey his commandments; should I trespass, it will not be through ignorance. And we argue endlessly (with growing delectation) over metrics.

As I understand it, he usually chooses either a very rigid formality or a very loose free verse; I tend to fall between those stools—or, if you will, trapeze bars. Writing formal verse, I try to push traditional forms to the breaking point; he keeps rules. (This may partly explain why he seldom writes metrical verse now.) In free verse, on the other hand, he may forgo all sense of local control and pattern; I often use any freedoms I take just to create new formalities, new patterns. In metre, I read and re-read Wyatt and Donne; in free verse, "Out of the Cradle." I imagine that Don reads Spencer and Sydney in metred verse, "Song of Myself" in free. The constants, then, are his predilection for a simpler, more placid surface, mine for a turbulent musical texture. His hope is to let a deep, less obvious music and meaning rise through the calmer surface; his danger, that this quieter surface remains unaided if those depths fail. My hope is that a complicated, more melodramatic surface may lend richness; the danger, that this turbulence can stifle or replace the deeper music.

There are similar disparities between our broader vital strategies: his life often seemed stolid and settled one year, wild and giddy the next; mine was usually somewhere between. He is alternately burgher and outlaw; I try both at once. One year, he turns in at 8:30 every night and is patiently miffed if you phone ten minutes after sundown; next year, you can't get him on the phone at all—he has just joined the Pittsburgh Pirates' training camp and is out all night every night with the Dallas Cheerleaders. I go to bed at 2 a.m., having told a stimulating anecdote to a friend's wife.

In any case, Don's rigid metrics (trying as I then was to develop my "ear,") helped sour me on his early poems. But what could I tell him? I didn't want to lose a friend—certainly not one who liked my work. All artists, of course, face such problems. Our cold war literary world, with its cliques and power gangs, its treaties and secret deals, its backscratchings and backbitings, betrays that most of us readily scrap our opinions in favor of advantage. Still, I can't help hoping, even believing, that some find more courage—more than I did.

I resorted to the lie—at best, gross exaggeration—that I hadn't read his poems: neurotic compulsions kept me from reading scarcely any poetry. This last was true; but I *had* read Don's poems. The dilemma sharpened when we came to live near each other. I took a job at Wayne State Univ. in Detroit; Don taught at the Univ. of Michigan, 40 miles away. This threw us together at poetry readings, parties, plays, concerts. Then we started playing tennis. It got harder, but all the more imperative, to maintain my fiction of not knowing his work.

Little by little, though, over the years, I did find pieces I honestly admired. First, I stumbled onto *String Too Short to Be Saved*, the prose sketches of his family and their rural New England neighbors. I was specially touched by the stories about his grandfather, Wesley Wells—the same grandfather whose house and farm he now inhabits. Now, I could talk about *some* of his work; need I describe my relief? And, since those were prose pieces, I could keep the pretense of not knowing the poems.

Again, as we sat talking before parties or after tennis, I began to find unsuspected depths. I was used to the Donald Hall who played the clown or philistine, told "knock-knock" jokes, talked gibberish everyone mistook for Russian, played the role of Père Ubu (Papa Poopy, the usurper king of Poland); I did not expect profundity. I was anxious to spout my theories about modernism to anyone in the field. He not only took my seismic revelations calmly; he knew things, astonishing things, I had never considered. I urged him to set those ideas on paper but he seemed no more impressed with *his* ideas than with mine. Or perhaps he just couldn't get excited about criticism at all. To turn our mental soccer matches into career enhancements — the American way — may have seemed boring.

And in time, I *did* find poems, too, that I liked — pieces I'd have liked if they'd appeared under the name of Sam Blffrfswtz. And, oddly enough, just as those fine first stories concerned the grandfather about whom he has since written so much, so well, the poems that first hooked me often broached subjects decisive in his later work. This may not prove the excellence of those poems; it mightily suggests that at least one of us has been actively obsessed by those themes.

Among the first of those is a sort of *ars poetica* which deals, even in its title, with an attitude toward time:

THE DAYS

Ten years ago this minute, he possibly sat
in the sunlight, in Connecticut, in an old chair:
a car may have stopped in the street outside;
he may have turned his head; his ear may have itched.
Since it was September, he probably saw
single leaves dropping from the maple tree.

If he was reading, he turned back to his book,
and perhaps the smell of roses in a pot
came together with the smell of cheese sandwiches
and the smell of a cigarette
smoked by his brother who was not dead then.

The moments of that day dwindled
to the small notations of clocks,
and the day busily became another day,
and another, and today, when his hand moves
from his ear which still itches
to rest on his leg, it is marked with the passage
of ten years. Suddenly he has the idea
that thousands and thousands of his days
lie stacked into the ground
like leaves, or like that pressure of green
which turns into coal in a million years.

Though leaves rot, or leaves burn in the gutter;
though the complications of this morning's breakfast
dissolve in faint shudders of light
at a great distance, he continues to daydream
that the past is a country under the ground
where the days practice their old habits
over and over, as faint and persistent
as cigarette smoke in an airless room.
He wishes he could travel there like a tourist
and photograph the unseizable days
in the sunlight, in Connecticut, in an old chair.

This fascination with the past, its accretion and preservation, with the possibility of its recovery and transformation, appears often. It might turn up among the dilemmas of the living in more threatening shapes:

THE MAN IN THE DEAD MACHINE

High on a slope in New Guinea
the Grumman Hellcat

lodges among bright vines
as thick as arms. In 1942,
the clenched hand of a pilot
glided it here
where no one has ever been.

In the cockpit the helmeted
skeleton sits
upright, held
by dry sinews at neck
and shoulder, and webbing
that straps the pelvic cross
to the cracked
leather of the seat, and the breastbone
to the canvas cover
of the parachute.
Or say that the shrapnel
missed me, I flew
back to the carrier, and every morning
take my train, my pale
hands on a black case, and sit
upright, held
by the firm webbing.

This offers, among other things, an image of life in victorious, imperial America — where even the victorious are trapped like flies in the web of a voracious and life-draining system.

A third poem, like so many later, is not about being devoured but about eating, about a different kind of accretion, an appetite for experience which lets one (as artist or human) escape that fearful webbing and turn his days into a Protean, if absurd, animal vitality.

SELF-PORTRAIT, AS A BEAR

Here is a fat animal, a bear
that is partly a dodo.
Ridiculous wings hang at his shoulders

> as if they were collarbones
> while he plods in the bad brickyards
> at the edge of the city smiling
> and eating flowers. He eats them
> because he loves them
> because they are beautiful
> because they love him.
> It is eating flowers which makes him fat.
> He carries his huge stomach
> over the gutters of damp leaves
> in the parking lots in October,
> but inside that paunch
> he knows there are fields of lupine
> and meadows of mustard and poppy.
> He encloses sunshine.
> Winds bend the flowers
> in combers across the valley,
> birds hang on the stiff wind,
> at night there are showers, and the sun
> lifts through a haze every morning
> of the summer in the stomach.

A bear? With wings? A dodo? Like many fixed on an unalterable course, Don could seem unstable, could assume many guises. Who knew whether he would come to the party as a bear or a dodo, as Don Giovanni or Don Meredith, as Jack Armstrong or Jackie Gleason?

A fat animal? Like many former athletes, like many who have kept sharp appetites, Don—who had been slimmer, more muscular than I—was tending toward a grosser embodiment of "summer in the stomach." At tennis now, he would gasp and sputter after difficult shots, his face a darkening red. I sometimes feared a good return might rob me of my partner and our literature one of its best practitioners. (An idle, self-congratulatory fear: my prowess threatened no man's apoplexy.)

Eating flowers? Because *they* love *him?* Like many lovers of beauty, like many who've had closely restricted childhoods, he was developing a sort of Don Juanism toward experience. One advantage of a proper childhood (aside from the greater chance that you will grow up at all) is that you will probably grow up dissatisfied. This can offer a richer, more various life — or a wasted one. In this affluent, post-Augustan society, we can change (or evade) commitments, can remain adolescent — for good reasons or bad — terribly late. Maturity has its pitfalls; adulthood without it, no less.

Once when I had lured him to courtside to sit and drain the crimson from his visage, he compared our lives to that of some of the athletes he knew. The competition between us, of course, is absolutely crucial to our lives. Competition gets a bad press these days — it often does among those who've had comfort dropped in their laps. But those embraces between boxers who have just spent an hour bashing each other's faces in, bespeak a real gratitude. It would be a sorrier place without his criticism or the threat of his example. Over the years, he is almost the only poet I've like giving readings with — on *that* court there's no danger (and no hope) that some stroke of mine will drive him into apoplexy, despair or silence. Reading with him, there's one answer: read better than you're able.

He also remarked how much luckier we are than athletes — we get about the same amount of productive time; theirs, though, is compacted into a mere 15 years or so. They can't reconsider or seriously falter; they're washed up by 35. Thank God, he said, ours is strung out in short bursts over a lifetime. For us, being neurotic, starting over, changing our approach, may be of the essence. Like many artists, we have both been neurotic, uncertain, have started over and over. And though,

I think, basically monogamous, we've both had periods of recur-
rent adolescence, turmoil, pursuit and divorce. Typically, his
have been more dramatic; mine, almost habitual.

His life began changing, of course, well before his divorce.
After it, changes become not merely apparent, but manifold,
nearly mythic. If I tried to call him in Ann Arbor, I'd find that
he, with a group of professional friends, actually *had* joined the
Pittsburgh Pirates' training camp in Florida. Or he was in California living in Elsa Lanchester's house. When I *did* run into him—
at parties, at poetry readings, at play rehearsals or, more per-
ilously, at home—the megavoltage of his activities left me
anxious I might soon find him in an employment line, jail cell
or emergency ward. One year, at the first meeting of his modern
poetry seminar, he tried to announce that the class would meet,
thereafter, at his home. Instead, he declared, "From now on,
this class will meet in my bedroom." Even *he* was worried that
no one seemed surprised.

The designation of "home," itself, changed surprisingly. Since
he had first come to Ann Arbor, Don had lived in a small,
battered house on a comfortable side street. As his position
solidified, he had bought and moved into a fine big house from
a former college president. How many marriages break up at
just such a moment! Next thing I knew, he was in a tiny
graduate-style apartment, living on what he could make on
readings and free-lancing. Meantime, he gave my third wife and
myself demonstrations of gourmet bread-slicing: producing, free-
hand, slices so thin I could have passed them through my
typewriter.

This did not alleviate his weight problem as much as one
might expect—perhaps because he was, steadily, becoming a
skillful businessman, an adept literary and academic politician.

This, no doubt, made indulgence in other gourmet practices possible once again. I sometimes wondered if he had needed a divorce, as Ibsen seemed to need a demanding wife, to insure his own productivity? In no time, he had moved back into the original small, battered house on its comfortable side street.

It had never occurred to me that one could earn a living by writing. (Had I thought so, I might never have become a writer; some part of me was once as opposed to profit as it was to winning tennis matches.) Don, on the other hand, said that when he got together with other poets, they did not talk about metrics, rhetoric or imagery, but about tax loopholes. I cannot vouch for the creativity of his tax forms; I was amazed at the amount of profitable hack work he found and the excellence of things he turned out. The visits to the baseball camps produced *Playing Around* and *Fathers Playing Catch with Sons*. The visits to Elsa Lanchester produced a book about her husband, Charles Laughton — which she had initiated but then would not permit to appear. His other books turn up everywhere: my wife teaches from *Writing Well*; I use *Claims for Poetry* and *Remembering Poets*, not to mention his various anthologies.

In no time, Don was making twice what I could from readings, meantime turning out columns, reviews, anthologies, textbooks, stage pieces, books on Henry Moore, Dock Ellis and (now, again, recently contracted for) Charles Laughton. He began to look less like a dead fly in the web of American business, than a sheepdog badgering a herd of typists — one for letters, one for texts and anthologies, a third for reviews and columns, still another for stories and poems. I would get letters dictated to a hand-held Sony while he drove through far corners of the country. And his business sense came, from time to time, to my aid. Learning that I needed money because of my own divorce and an impending trip to the Balkans, he wangled a large advance for me to do three books with his publisher. Two of those actually appeared.

I tried often, less successfully, to repay his help. I was once approached to head a large writers' workshop that had long been run by a man of fierce political skill and determination but who had finally amassed too many enemies. Tied down by my psychoanalysis in Detroit, I suggested Don — a better poet than the past head and almost as adept at academic politics. Vaguely uncomfortable about the job, he told his hosts he couldn't take it because the former director would still be on the grounds. Thereupon, without asking Don, they told the older man he'd have to leave at once and reoffered the post to Don. At this point, he realized the true reason: between advances and grants, he might not have to teach at all for three or four years! In the long run, I think everyone benefitted, but things were sticky for a while, especially for those colleagues who now had to ask their departing boss to please come back — but only for a year!

Even while his life was undergoing these obvious changes, so was his poetic style. The discursive voice and formal metrics of *Exiles and Marriages* (1955) had opened out into the syllabics and free verse of *The Dark Houses* and *A Roof of Tiger Lilies* (1964), moving on into occasional near-surrealism in *The Alligator Bride* (1969). This in turn gave way to the clipped lines and compressed diction of *The Yellow Room* (1971). In the small volume, *The Town of Hill* (1975), we find, side by side, such disparate styles as the short lines and factual voice of the title poem (a redaction of a passage from Ovid), the formality of "Eleanor's Letters," the phantasmagoric prose-poetry of "The Presidentiad" or the open free verse of the hilarious "To a

Waterfowl." I witnessed some of these stylistic changes, like the personal ones, with alarm, though I could see that splendid poems were accumulating and should have seen that the present turmoil involved, both in theme and style, re-examining what to save of one's past. Poetically, I think, such maturity arrived only with *Kicking the Leaves* (1978) but its bounty amply justified whatever experiments led to it.

As suggested, this stylistic maturity coincides with his marriage to Jane Kenyon and the move to New Hampshire. *Kicking the Leaves* contains poems set in both locations and one, "Maple Syrup," is about introducing his wife to that landscape. After looking unsuccessfully for his grandfather's grave, the couple do find in the cellar a quart of maple syrup the old man had made twenty-five years before:

> I remember
> coming to the farm in March
> in sugaring time, as a small boy.
> He carried the pails of sap, sixteen-quart
> buckets, dangling from each end
> of a wooden yoke
> that lay across his shoulders, and emptied them
> into a vat in the saphouse
> where fire burned day and night
> for a week.
> Now the saphouse
> tilts, nearly to the ground,
> like someone exhausted
> to the point of death, and next winter
> when snow piles three feet thick
> on the roofs of the cold farm,
> the saphouse will shudder and slide
> with the snow to the ground.

<blockquote>
<pre>
                    Today
    we take my grandfather's last
    quart of syrup
    upstairs, holding it gingerly,
    and we wash off twenty-five years
    of dirt, and we pull
    and pry the lid up, cutting the stiff
    dried rubber gasket, and dip our fingers
    in, you and I both, and taste
    the sweetness, you for the first time,
    the sweetness preserved, of a dead man
    in his own kitchen,
    giving us
    from his lost grave the gift of sweetness.
</pre>
</blockquote>

Though images both of leaves and of photographs, as earlier in "The Days," appear in splendid poems here (e.g., "Kicking the Leaves" and "Photographs of China"), this jar seems to me a better vessel for the passing and preservation of our tenuous existence, a sturdier *ars poetica.*

Other poems, here, also deal with eating, with hunger and food: "Maple Syrup," "Eating the Pig," "O Cheese." Perhaps the most powerful is "Wolf Knife" which recounts the adventure of a Navy explorer, travelling by dog sledge with his Eskimo guide across the frozen Crispin Bay. When two wolves begin tracking them, the guide fixes, upright in the snow, two razor-sharp *turnoks*, Eskimo knives, wet with the blood of a sled dog he has just killed. Amost at once the two wolves begin licking the knives so that

<blockquote>
<pre>
        ". . . their own blood poured
    copiously forth
    to replenish the dog's blood, and they ate
    more furiously than before, while Kantiuk laughed,
    and held his sides
    laughing.
</pre>
</blockquote>

"And I laughed also,
perhaps in relief that Providence had delivered us
yet again, or perhaps — under conditions of extremity,
far from Connecticut — finding these creatures
acutely ridiculous, so avid
to swallow their own blood. First one, and then the other
collapsed, dying
bloodless in the snow black with their own blood,
and Kantiuk retrieved
his *turnoks*, and hacked lean meat
from the thigh of the larger wolf,
which we ate
gratefully, blessing the Creator, for we were hungry."

The explorer's piety of language, which protects him from seeing his essential likeness to the wolves or that he and his guide, ultimately, devour their own blood, gives the passage a strength beyond the reach of any "tougher" language, beyond the scope of any commentary.

The young dog Kantiuk killed in that poem

". . . had yowled, moaned, and now lay
expiring, surrounded
by curious cousins and uncles,
possibly hungry . . ."

Still, Don has chosen an existence and an expiration "surrounded by curious cousins and uncles." Though we, too, are carnivores, though the skeleton (like the dead pilot in his dead machine) sits at our feast, the speaker of these poems responds to a greater hunger, not for the flesh, but for the re-imagined lives of his forebears. He lives in their house, attends their church, observes their rituals, traces their leavings. There, too, he moves with the daily, weekly, yearly, seasonal round of the farm, the family, the village, the landscape. He writes in "Stone Walls":

> At Church we eat squares of bread, we commune with
>   mothers
> and cousins, with mothering-fathering hills, with dead
>   and living
> and go home in gray November, in Advent waiting,
> among generations unborn
> who will look at the same hills . . .
> I grow old, in the house I wanted to grow old in.
> When I am sleepy at night, I daydream only
> of waking the next morning—to walk on the earth of
>   the present
> past noons of birch and sugarbush, past cellarholes,
> many miles to the village of nightfall.

Only so is the fact of death acceptable, even welcome. I cannot resist quoting intact the marvelous last section of "Kicking the Leaves":

> Now I fall, now I leap and fall
> to feel the leaves crush under my body, to feel my body
> buoyant in the ocean of leaves, the night of them,
> night heaving with death and leaves, rocking like the ocean.
> Oh, this delicious falling into the arms of leaves,
> into the soft laps of leaves!
> Face down I swim into the leaves, feathery,
> breathing the acrid odor of maple, swooping
> in long glides to the bottom of October—
> where the farm lies curled against winter, and soup steams
> its breath of onion and carrot
> onto damp curtains and windows; and past the windows
> I see the tall bare maple trunks and branches, the oak
> with its few brown weathery remnant leaves,
> with the spruce trees, holding their green.
> Now I leap and fall, exultant, recovering
> from death, on account of death, in accord with the dead,
> the smell and taste of leaves again,
> and the pleasure, the only long pleasure, of taking a place
> in the story of leaves.

That story informs poem after poem here: "Flies," "The Black Faced Sheep," "Ox Cart Man," "Old Roses," "Names of Horses" or "Stone Walls." It is hard to resist quoting them all.

Despite these poems, despite the younger poets and readers across the country quoting them, the opinion makers hear nothing. Don's present neglect, of course, attaches directly to his past influence. Some will never forgive you for having held powers they wanted; some will never forgive themselves that they once praised your work.

Now that his business and political savvy have enabled him to leave, more or less, the literary and academic bargain marts, he seems to have become careless of Po-Biz. He never did join the Genius of the Month Club, dared openly dissent on several poets we are currently required to revere. He praised the book of a younger poet who had sourly dispraised one of his. (When they met at a conference, the younger man expressed embarassment about his own review; this did not prevent him from savaging Don's next book.) He told the most powerful American critic, face to face, that for the good of American letters, that critic should stop writing.

Can he believe such acts will not have consequences? Whole networks of critics, coteries, magazines, power groups and lobbyists could lose dominion. Such acts remain subject to a principle defined for me by Constance Urdang: No Good Deed Shall Go Unpunished.

You could almost believe he had found something more important—a place among the leaves, the animals, the neighborhood, the spirits of ancestors. A place, for instance at Eagle Pond where—having passed by Jan, Jen, Gin, Jean, Joan and June—one might go with Jane: a pilgrimage worth making. Many years ago, in Detroit, during another pause in a tennis game, Don remarked that when he was young, there were only two things that he really loved: poetry and kissing. He thought it ironic that he'd spent his time with young women who liked neither. Well, whatever Jane Kenyon may think of kissing, we know what she thinks about poetry. Or we read *The Boat of Quiet Hours*; the calm warmth of those poems is honestly come by.

For several years, Don and Jane, my third wife and I would make up a foursome for a lesser pilgrimage to the Stratford Ont. festival; we visited back and forth in each other's farmhouses in New Hampshire and New York state. Once, driving to our house near Erieville, N.Y., Don and Jane were caught in a blizzard; they phoned to say they'd had to stop 15 miles away because the roads were so slippery. I jumped in my jeep and went to pick them up, telling them as we whisked along how one needn't fear skids in a four-wheel-drive vehicle. Those words were scarcely out when the jeep began revolving slowly like a Dodgem car, finally oozing off the road to rest in a field of corn stocks. They have never again mentioned that episode; they acted, then, as if there were nothing frightening or humorous about my claims to expertise. It is well to have passed such slithery voyagings, to have reached a destination, secure because so well anchored in one's past.

Now, both Don and I are so driven by deadlines that we can seldom drive to see each other, but that is like the short bursts of productivity he saw in the artist's life. We still give poetry readings together — and I am astonished at how he has changed — we're both almost slim again and as solidly married as anyone is like to be in this culture. Don drinks little, goes to bed early and never answers his telephone at all. Mostly, though, we've resorted to letters, the way we first got to know each other—less fun but perhaps richer. If my life fell apart tomorrow, I would know who to tell; if my health wobbled, Don would welcome me (he recently *did*) into the Aging Poets' Diabetic and Child Bride Association.

In New Hampshire, they live not happily ever after—who lives, even miserably, ever after?—but industriously *while* they live. Outside, the farmhouse looks cozy; inside, it rambles like a shopping mall. Jane, given the single bent of her writing, spends much of her day in the third floor's far corner. There, out of sight and earshot, in a spacious, sun-splashed studio, she works on poems. Don, moving from poems to short stories, then to reviews, columns, textbooks, anthologies or finally to his voluminous correspondence, progresses from desk to desk in domestic heliotropism through the rest of the house. One of his desks—a big roll-top made of old Honduran mahogany— he bought from my third wife. There, I try to tell myself, he works on poems. So I can feel somehow involved in such an important enterprise. And can envy those poems a little less.

There is much to envy. Sections of *The One Day*—the long poem he has been fashioning for more than ten years—are now appearing in the journals and in *The Happy Man* (1986), his latest book of poems. These previews, foreshocks of quakes and upheavals, suggest that California is not the only land-scape soon to change; poetry's Richter Scale may have to be extended.

After many years, I finally did get nerve to tell Don I had known his poems all along but simply hadn't liked the early ones. Of course he had always known. But how, I asked, did he ever manage that—to go on supporting my work, publicly and privately—I don't think I know anyone else who could have done that. Look, he said, if you had liked those poems it wouldn't have made them one bit better than they were; your disliking them didn't make them one bit worse.

Lots of people *tell* you things like that.

DONALD'S WAY

❧ Louis Simpson ☙

In the winter of 1954 I submitted a poem to *The Paris Review*. The poetry editor, Donald Hall, wrote back accepting the poem and suggesting a change. I had written:

> . . . hands looked thin
> Around a cigarette that, like an ember,
> Would pulse . . .

He said that a lighted cigarette *was* an ember. I revised the line to read:

> Around a cigarette, and the bright ember

This was the beginning of our friendship. For thirty-three years we have been friends and critics of each other's work. It has been mostly practical criticism, having to do with the meaning, form, and sound of poems. But sometimes we have argued about ideas and attitudes.

I recall one blazing quarrel over Ezra Pound. Donald had once interviewed Pound. In my book *Three on the Tower* I remarked that the interviewer had not broached the matter of Pound's Fascism and anti-Semitism. Donald protested that he had, and cited some sentences from the interview. I said that they were so mild that no one would have noticed. From this the argument escalated, sending people out of the room.

We have often agreed to differ. We like each other—that's

the important thing. When I'm in his company I feel happy —
his talk is full of fun. Like Falstaff, whom Donald used to resemble before he went on a diet, he is not only witty in himself
but a cause that wit is in other men. That is, he makes you
think you are witty.

In 1956 Robert Pack, Donald, and I put together an anthology
of verse. It was Pack's idea and he came up with the funding.
Donald was living near Boston — he was a Junior Fellow at
Harvard. The three editors would meet at his house or my
apartment in Manhattan. We read a large number of American
and English poets, the English being presented by Donald who
had studied at Oxford. We made some happy discoveries. I recall
how earnestly Donald and I argued for including poems by W.D.
Snodgrass, poems Snodgrass later published in *Heart's Needle*.
There were others — Adrienne Rich, Denise Levertov. W.S.
Merwin, Robert Bly, James Wright — who were not well known
at the time. *The New Poets of England and America* helped to
make them so. We left out two or three poets who should have
been included, but if we made mistakes no one could accuse
us of playing literary politics — we chose poetry we liked without
considering the author.

And so we made not a few enemies. Poets who had been left
out said that the anthology was academic and they were the
avant-garde. They got together an anthology of their own, *The
New American Poetry*. Now, thirty years later, some of the "new
American poets" look very old — they have even become mem-
bers of the American Academy and Institute of Arts and Letters.

Besides being a poet and playwright, Donald is an editor,
anthologist, writer of textbooks, reviewer, and literary journalist.
I don't know any other man or woman who has done as much
to bring the best contemporary writing to the attention of the

public. And I can only estimate, by what he has done for me, how much he has done for his friends or for strangers. He once sent me five pages, single spaced, of criticisms of a book I was about to publish. Several of his criticisms saved me from making a fool of myself.

There is one kind of journalism I wish he wouldn't do, and I have told him so: articles about the "state of poetry," how many poetry readings took place last year, how many copies of a book were sold, et cetera. These articles are depressing because they have nothing to do with poetry, the feelings one has about it. Who on earth are such articles written for? Writing about poetry business is no occupation for a poet. I told him so on a road near his house in Danbury, and we argued the matter in voices that sent birds flying out of the trees.

He is first of all a poet. I have been reading his poems since *Exiles and Marriages*, the book *Time* said might win a Pulitzer prize. This made some poets angry — they would have preferred to have it said about them. Donald has written much better poems since that first book, and he has yet to be awarded one of the big prizes. Critics who look for something new may well turn their attention to the poetry Donald Hall has written since moving to New Hampshire. It is a body of work like no other — he is a trend all to himself. One could think that he is lucky to have this landscape and these people to write about, but he managed the luck, living where he does and writing until he found a manner of his own.

He has not come to it easily, and from time to time he reverts to the facetious English manner of some early poem — one hears dons laughing in the Common Room. In the poem "O Cheese" in *Kicking the Leaves*, for example . . .

> Pont l' Evêque intellectual, and quite well informed;
>   Emmentaler
> decent and loyal, a little deaf in the right ear;
> and Brie the revealing experience, instantaneous and
>   profound.

It is impossible to read these lines without hearing the voice of the snob, the kind of person who uses words like "decent and loyal . . . revealing experience, instantaneous and profound," in order to be amusing.

But *Kicking the Leaves* and *The Happy Man* provide many instances of something quite different, poems about life and death, in a style both grave and humorous that is most appealing. On the surface they are poems about country living, and will be taken as such by many readers, but this is only the surface. They are about the changing seasons of human life, the movement from youth to old age and death, the passing of life from one generation to another. They are infused with pity for the living and one might almost say envy of the dead. This is where Hall's peculiar courage comes in. The insincere poet, the one who is inventing a persona he thinks the public will like, working from whatever is fashionable in politics or psychology, would not write such poems. They reveal what the poet really is, what he really likes, whether others like it or not. Hall presents his heart's affections as if they were holy, and makes them seem so.

He doesn't hold it against the dead that they have died. He still likes their company and walks alongside a father and mother, a grandfather, as though they were as alive and worthy of liking as ever. He isn't afraid of the past . . . that is to say, he isn't afraid of being human, knowing that he too will die.

> Now I leap and fall, exultant, recovering
> from death, on account of death, in accord with the dead,
> the smell and taste of leaves again,
> and the pleasure, the only long pleasure, of taking a place
> in the story of leaves.

> (from *Kicking the Leaves*)

His affection extends to animals — his poems about them are memorable: "The Black Faced Sheep," "Names of Horses," "Great Day in the Cow' House," "The Henyard Round." He deals with animals as country people do . . . realistically. We are spared none of their stupidity. But he likes them too:

> When the shearer cut to your nakedness in April
> and you dropped black eyes in shame,
> hiding in barnyard corners, unable to hide,
> I brought grain to raise your spirits . . .

> (from *The Black Faced Sheep*)

It is clear as we read these poems that they aren't just about cows, sheep, and chickens but about all of us. The shorn sheep are like Adam and Eve after the fall, hiding their shame, and the poet is the angel who brings them comfort. These barnyard poems have a Biblical ring. We are observing the human condition, seen clearly for what it is, and with a certain forgiveness. All his best qualities are in the poem "Stone Walls" — his love of the seasons, the land, his grandfather Wesley Wells, the animals. His pleasure in anecdote . . .

> Lawyer Green, whose skin was the color green,
> ridiculed as a schoolboy, who left town and returned
> triumphant . . . .

His turning of anecdote into something more permanent,
history . . . .

> how he walked on a row of fenceposts
> in the blizzard of eighty-eight . . . .

And his own, personal history . . . how he went to school and
dreamed of another, more feeling life with his grandfather. He
likes the land best in November when:

> the brightness washes from the hills
> . . . leaves down, color drained out
> in November rain,
> everything gray and brown . . . .

"Stone Walls" seems absolutely real: the description in words
is as real as the land itself, and the feeling makes it so.

    Kicking the Leaves and *The Happy Man* have given us poems
that make the landscape of Kearsarge and Ragged Mountain
part of our interior landscape. Not only the land . . . the people:

> At Thornley's Store,
> the dead mingle with the living; Benjamin Keneston hovers
> with Wesley among hardware; Kate looks over spools of
>   thread
> with Nanny, and old shadows stand among dowels and
>   raisins,
> woolen socks and axes. Now Ansel stops to buy salt
> and tells Bob Thornley it got so cold he saw
> two hounddogs put jumper cables on a jackrabbit.

> (from *Stone Walls*)

    Poems such as these are rare, but they make us think that
the life of poetry is worthwhile.

DONALD HALL'S HOUSE
OF VIRTUE BUILT IN THE WOODS
AND FIELDS OF TIME

Hayden Carruth

Throughout Donald Hall's writing the aspect of personal elegy has been predominant. His first popular book, *String Too Short to Be Saved* (1961), which has been recently republished and remains popular today, is an account in prose of his grandparents' farm in Wilmot, New Hampshire, as he knew it when he was a boy, a discourse on the values represented by his grandparents' generation of rural Americans, also on the values of his parents' generation—they lived in southern Connecticut and were basically urban professionals—and on the impact of all these conflicting understandings upon the mind of a boy growing up in the 1930s and 1940s.

And these have been the persisting, almost obsessive concerns evinced in all his writing for more than thirty years: poetry, fiction, literary essays, and even in his newspaper and magazine articles about sports, travel, and anything else he has been able to think of that might sell. Hall has supported himself and his family as a free-lance writer and editor for a long time. Autobiography, in the broadest sense of the term, has been his bread and butter. Maybe he was influenced by Lowell, Berryman, Jarrell, Shapiro, and others of that group—Hall's first book of poems, *Exiles and Marriages* (the title is exact), was published in 1955, only a couple of years after Lowell's *Life Studies*, and Hall is a Harvard graduate, a New Englander oriented toward Cambridge and Boston—but I don't see a necessary connection, and in any case many of Hall's contemporaries—Plath, Merwin, Rich, Kinnell, Creeley, Berry, and scores of others—were only doing the same things. After the programmatic impersonalism of much of the modernist movement between the two big wars, autobiography was, so to speak, in the air. Relationships within families, between families and locations, among conflicting ages and cultures and sexes: these became the staples of American poetry after mid-century, as we all know.

And we know the dangers of elegiac autobiography: nostalgia, sentimentality, and ultra-subjectivism or solipsism. These are customarily said to be diseases; they infect and weaken the human spirit. Myself, I'm not so sure of this, as I've argued elsewhere. But whatever the merits of that argument, if nostalgia, sentimentality, and subjectivism are diseases, then so is being a writer, especially a poet, in our time. Nostalgia, sentiment, and the self are what we all write about almost all the time. Perhaps we can say that the dominant cultural traits of any era are the diseases of the human spirit which must be accepted and transcended by the writers of that era if they are to succeed, e.g. Whitman's progressivism and optimism (with which he wrote the greatest elegy in American literature), Pope's rationalism and pan-deism (with which he wrote the greatest mock-epic in English literature), and Dante's Thomistic, not to say Gothic, determinism (with which he wrote the greatest humane lyric of all time).

Those who survive a disease are those who have felt it most—Marcel Proust wrote: "Illness is the most heeded of doctors: to

kindness and wisdom we make promises only; pain we obey" —
and those who have transcended it — George Dennison has written: "Perhaps all sufferers are victims, but victimization cannot
create a figure of suffering; there must be some principle of
transcendence — courage, persistence, endurance — for otherwise
the sufferer has collapsed and does not represent suffering, but
defeat." Most of the poetry of our time registers nothing but
defeat. But more than courage, persistence, and endurance, I
think, though these are necessary, must go into real transcending. Dennison has also written of "the imperishability of
the boundary at which consciousness becomes aware of itself
gazing at the inexplicable." *This* is transcendence, just as it is
the limit of transcendence. To survive is not only to reach that
boundary but to live there. I don't think it can be reached
through nostalgia, sentimentality, and subjectivism, which, col-
lectively misnamed faith, are all that religion and patriotism,
our famous American instant cures for everything, can offer;
and courage and persistence are only elements of subjectivism.
To live at the boundary, to create a figure of suffering, a figure
of passion, is to live in history, including the future, and in the
mind of the species, not simply in one's own mind.

I would say 99% of current poetry I have read is written in
the present tense and the first person, both the tense and the
pronoun signifying one consciousness, compacted and odd. No
wonder young poets speak of one poem being "more unique"
than another.

A couple of weeks ago I drove from Utica to the interior of
Maine, where I am now, and I stopped in Wilmot to spend a
night with Donald Hall and Jane Kenyon; we have been friends
for some time, and both of them are writers whose work is
important in my life. (As it happens they have each published

two fine books in the past year: Kenyon's translations from Ahkmatova, the best we have in English, also her new book of poems, *The Boat of Quiet Hours*, and then Hall's books of stories and poems, *The Ideal Bakery* and *The Happy Man*.) The drive from Utica to Wilmot is depressing and much of it is infuriating: the poverty and desuetude of the Mohawk Valley, the tawdriness of Albany and Troy, the prettified gentility of towns like Manchester and Arlington in Vermont, the expensive ugliness of ski resorts, and so on, which doesn't mean that sections of honest farmland and functional year-round villages can't still be found. Wilmot, where the main line of the Hall family has lived in the same farmhouse for five generations, with cognate branches in nearby houses and towns, is such a place, though the developers are already at work there, inevitably, as the mess in eastern Massachusetts spreads outward in all directions, bulldozing woods and knolls, throwing up their pressed-wood condos and town houses, so alien to the genius of the New England countryside and, as far as I can see, to the human spirit generally.

I had read Jane's and Don's new books. This is not the place to review them. They are splendid books and contain genuinely authentic and important work. At least three of the stories in *The Ideal Bakery* are as good as any short fiction I know, and the poems in *The Happy Man* are clear, strong, original, beautifully voiced and cadenced, and they give me a good deal of pleasure. But what struck me most in these books, as it has struck me in nearly everything I've read in recent years, work by my students, my colleagues, my friends, myself, and all those others out there whose writing comes to me one way or another, is the elegiac mode of thought and feeling, the governing elegiac *gestalten* in all our imaginative attitudes. Tragic or comic, journalistic or surrealistic, witty or earnest, we can't write about anything except the things that are fading from our lives. This is the predicament of the young as well as the old, the westerners as well as the easterners, of everyone. Science fiction and spy fiction are full of elegy; poetry the same; it's a constant in television and the movies. We are the saddest people on earth. I suspect we are the saddest people who have ever been on earth. This is what I said to Jane and Don when I was in Wilmot, and they agreed. Everyone agrees.

Since then I have driven on into the north country where I've found the coves of rural poverty which are, for me, more beautiful than any of the "beautiful places," untidy (though by no means messy) farms, shacks and trailers, gravel pits and cut-over woods. Yes, plenty of spoliation, yet nature appears to be holding her own. (One needs to look closely to see the effects of the major pollutants, like acid rain.) I am living by a pond which I share with loons, cormorants, great herons, black-crowned night herons, king-fishers, ravens, warblers, turtles, porcupines, moose, bears, and many other creatures, including a few human ones. The only jealousy here is sexual and confined to youth. I haven't heard anyone insult anyone else. Trading is a sport, not a *casus belli*, meetings are held to reconfirm humane values, not to publicize the contentions of avarice, and in one week I have been the grateful recipient of more generosity than I've had in the whole past year as a member of the institutional academic community, which is not a community at all. Ollie North, goddamn his eyes, is the kind of posing, whining egomaniac who gets thrown out of the real communities in Maine.

But this is a backwater, literally. It is not Boothbay or Deer Isle. Not many places like this are left. The rest of the country, the rest of the civilization has been turned into a nightmare of greed and suffering. And what resources have we who are reflective personalities to fall back on except sentimentality, nostalgia, and our subjective identities? These have become not only our virtures but the substance of all our conversation, most of which is comic in intent. When twilight gathers in the wonderful foliage of the white ash trees, the swamp maples, the butternuts, the cedars, people gather together and their conversation falls and crests with laughter, magnanimity, and affection, like the tree swallows playing with a feather. This is what we do to preserve ourselves in our daily lives. But art is something else; it is not conversation.

Art is what transcends virtue. This is a radical new idea, but inescapable. Nostalgia, sentimentality, and subjectivity, though they are the flesh and bare bones of 99% of what is called poetry today, are only the beginnings of realized art, which is unanalysable and generally indescribable. Dante's love for Beatrice was nostalgic, sentimental, and subjective in the extreme, but it is the virtue that made possible the failure of mind and language that transcends itself in Dante's extraordinary final canto. The love, in other words, was only the beginning. In a very different but recognizable way, turning basic emotion into rightness, Donald Hall's best short stories do this too, like "The Figure of the Woods" and "The Ideal Bakery." But to my mind his three-part poem called The One Day is Hall's very best work.

The first part, "Shrubs Burned Away" (the title later changed to "Shrubs Burnt Away"), is contained in The Happy Man. The second part, "Four Classic Texts," I read in manuscript about a year ago. I was given the manuscript of the whole poem, revised and including the third part, "The One Day," when I visited

Wilmot. It is as completely right and natural and *there* as the laughter of the loons. At the same time it is as comprehensive, as transcending as any recent writing I know.

Commonly people say that a work of art is timeless. This is what workshop students believe, what they aim at with their constant reliance on the present tense and ridiculous participial phrasings. But a work of art eats time, consumes time, obliterating everything else. True, it can exist forever on a shelf or in a museum, but its meaning and essence become apparent only when it is functional in consciousness, in time, and then it is totally functional. *The One Day* contains many, probably most, of the materials in Hall's earlier work, his grandparents and parents, the farm, the people in his life today, his own thoughts and feelings about "marriage and exile" over the years, his education in classical literature, all his sentimentality and nostalgia and subjectivity, but it is not a summary of these things; far from it. It is a poem of the evolved human species from its beginning to its present to its end. And its language is not written but given. I don't mean this in a mystical sense, though Hall might. I mean that the language of this poem is given in the same way that the top of a mountain is given once you have climbed it. One knew it was there but not what it looked like.

Donald Hall is a public man. He was a teacher for a long time before he became a free lance, he frequently does readings and lectures, his critical and editorial work has made him a well-known person whose efforts on behalf of serious writing are widely appreciated. But he wrote *The One Day* in another compartment of his mind and sensibility entirely, in utter solitude, where the public man with his gestures and responses — which are the inverse of those of a private man, both having been created as diffractions of the ego from reality — is supplanted by simple undifferentiated heterogeneity, the consciousness of the womb or outer space, call it what one will, and where the world turns into the act of knowing. History is part of it inevitably, but so are all significant things — voices, dreams, places, especially a particular place, the house. Hall loves to show his visitors around his house in Wilmot, where every room and nearly every object have a tale attached, which he expounds with a kind of modest enthusiasm. His big poem is such a tour, but conducted as if by the voice of the house itself and all its objects, that is to say, by the world and all its history, apart from such human predicaments as pleasure and pain, intelligence and stupidity, yet expressive of a personality. And in the end we are reminded that personality is nothing but a structure of values.

So the poem, like all considerable works of art, moves circularly or, to state it more accurately, in a helix, a constantly rebounding ascent or transcent within the cylinder of consciousness hemmed in by the inexplicable. The human mind rising out of itself, content with ignorance, content with a faith that can in the full realization of our existential condition be nothing but perfunctory, but content as well with experience, our own inexplicable but undeniable being. *The One Day* is a complex, solid, and very habitable piece of work.

Donald Hall with his father, Donald Hall, Sr. at the beach in the summer
of 1929; and with his father in 1931

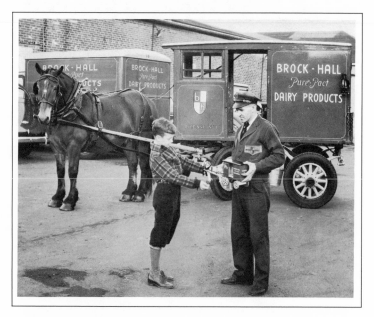

Donald Hall as a boy, from an ad printed in the Sunday edition of the
New Haven Register, 1934; Brock-Hall was the family business,
a processor-distributor of milk and ice cream

With his mother, Lucy Hall, and Zippy, about 1938

1953, Photo accompanied an article on Hall
in *Isis*, Oxford's weekly magazine

Hall trying out for the Pittsburgh Pirates, with Luke Wrenn *(left)*
in 1973 during the writing of *Fathers Playing Catch with Sons*

Robyn Brown

Family snapshot of Hall with his wife, the poet Jane Kenyon and his daughter, Philippa *(above)*; Jane with Ada in 1987 *(below)*

1955, Donald Hall holding his son, Andrew (*above*);
1976, Andrew holding his father (*below*)

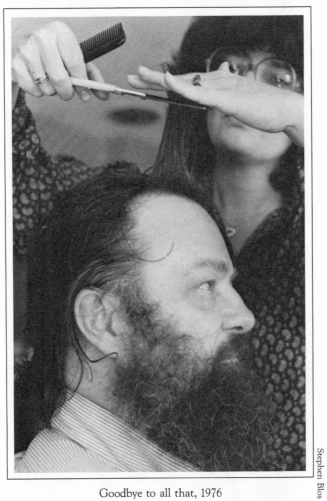

Goodbye to all that, 1976

15 POEMS BY
DONALD HALL

1953–1988

❧ Elegy For Wesley Wells

Against the clapboards and the window panes
The loud March whines with rain and heavy wind
In dark New Hampshire where his widow wakes.
She cannot sleep. The familiar length is gone.
I think across the clamorous Atlantic
To where the farm lies hard against the foot
Of Ragged Mountain, underneath Kearsarge.
The storm and hooded wind of equinox
Buffet against New England's bolted door
Across the sea and set the signals out
Eastport to Block Island.
I speak his name against the beating sea.

His dogs will whimper through the webby barn
Where spiders close his tools in a pale gauze
And wait for flies. The nervous woodchuck now
Will waddle plumply through the world of weeds
Eating wild peas as if he owned the land,
And the fat hedgehog rob the apple trees.
When next October's frosts harden the ground
And fasten in the year's catastrophe,
The farm will lie like driftwood,
The farmer dead, and deep in his carved earth.
Before the Civil War the land was used,
And railroads came to all the villages;
Before the war, a man with land was rich;
He cleared a dozen or two dozen acres,
Burning the timber, stacking up the stones,

And cultivated all his acreage
And planted it to vegetables to sell.
But then the war took off the hired men;
The fields grew up, to weeds and bushes first,
And then the fields were thick with ashy pine.
The faces of prosperity and luck
Turned westward with the railroads from New England.

Poverty settled, and the first went off,
Leaving their fathers' forty-acre farms,
To Manchester and Nashua and Lowell
And traded the Lyceum for the block.
Now the white houses fell, among the wars;
From eighteen-sixty-five, for eighty years,
The Georgian firmness sagged, and the paint chipped,
And the white houses rotted to the ground.
Great growths of timber felled grew up again
On what had once been cultivated land,
On lawns and meadows, and from cellar holes.
Deep in the forest now, half covered-up,
The reddened track of an abandoned railroad
Heaved in the frosts, in roots of the tall pines;
A locomotive stood
Like a strange rock, red as the fallen needles.

The farmer worked from four and milking time
To nine o'clock and shutting up the hens.
The heavy winter fattened him; the spring
Unlocked his arms and made his muscles lame.
By nineteen-forty, only the timid young
Remained to plough or sell.
He was the noble man in a sick place.

I number out the virtues that are dead,
Remembering the soft consistent voice
And bone that showed in each deliberate word.
I walk along old England's crowded shore
Where storm has driven everyone inside,
Ready to leave, to cross the hilly sea
And walk again among familiar hills
In dark New Hampshire where his widow wakes.
I think about the dead old man I loved,
The tall and straight bent in a clumsy box.
The length of Wesley Wells, those miles away,
Today was carried to the lettered plain
In Andover
While March bent down the cemetery trees.

❧ My Son, My Executioner

My son, my executioner,
   I take you in my arms,
Quiet and small and just astir,
   And whom my body warms.

Sweet death, small son, our instrument
   Of immortality,
Your cries and hungers document
   Our bodily decay.

We twenty-five and twenty-two,
   Who seemed to live forever,
Observe enduring life in you
   And start to die together.

❧ Christmas Eve in Whitneyville

December, and the closing of the year;
The momentary carolers complete
Their Christmas Eves, and quickly disappear
Into their houses on each lighted street.

Each car is put away in each garage;
Each husband home from work, to celebrate,
Has closed his house around him like a cage,
And wedged the tree until the tree stood straight.

Tonight you lie in Whitneyville again,
Near where you lived, and near the woods or farms
Which Eli Whitney settled with the men
Who worked at mass-producing firearms.

The main street, which was nothing after all
Except a school, a stable, and two stores,
Was improvised and individual,
Picking its way alone, among the wars.

Now Whitneyville is like the other places,
Ranch houses stretching flat beyond the square,
Same stores and movie, same composite faces
Speaking the language of the public air.

Old houses of brown shingle still surround
This graveyard where you wept when you were ten
And helped to set a coffin in the ground.
You left a friend from school behind you then,

And now return, a man of fifty-two.
Talk to the boy. Tell him about the years
When Whitneyville quadrupled, and how you
And all his friends went on to make careers,

Had cars as long as hayracks, boarded planes
For Rome or Paris where the pace was slow
And took the time to think how yearly gains,
Profit and volume made the business grow.

"The things I had to miss," you said last week,
"Or thought I had to, take my breath away."
You propped yourself on pillows, where your cheek
Was hollow, stubbled lightly with new gray.

This love is jail; another sets us free.
Tonight the houses and their noise distort
The thin rewards of solidarity.
The houses lean together for support.

The noises fail, and lights go on upstairs.
The men and women are undressing now
To go to sleep. They put their clothes on chairs
To take them up again. I think of how,

All over Whitneyville, when midnight comes,
They lie together and are quieted,
To sleep as children sleep, who suck their thumbs,
Cramped in the narrow rumple of each bed.

They will not have unpleasant thoughts tonight.
They make their houses jails, and they will take
No risk of freedom for the appetite,
Or knowledge of it, when they are awake.

The lights go out and it is Christmas Day.
The stones are white, the grass is black and deep.
I will go back and leave you here to stay
Where the dark houses harden into sleep.

The Long River

The musk-ox smells
in his long head
my boat coming. When
I feel him there,
intent, heavy,

the oars make wings
in the white night,
and deep woods are close
on either side
where trees darken.

I rowed past towns
in their black sleep
to come here. I rowed
by northern grass
and cold mountains.

The musk-ox moves
when the boat stops,
in hard thickets. Now
the wood is dark
with old pleasures.

✎ The Days

Ten years ago this minute, he possibly sat
in the sunlight, in Connecticut, in an old chair:
a car may have stopped in the street outside;
he may have turned his head; his ear may have itched.
Since it was September, he probably saw
single leaves dropping from the maple tree.
If he ws reading, he turned back to his book,
and perhaps the smell of roses in a pot
came together with the smell of cheese sandwiches
and the smell of a cigarette
smoked by his brother who was not dead then.

The moments of that day dwindled
to the small notations of clocks,
and the day busily became another day,
and another, and today, when his hand moves
from his ear which still itches
to rest on his leg, it is marked with the passage
of ten years. Suddenly he has the idea
that thousands and thousands of his days
lie stacked into the ground
like leaves, or like that pressure of green
which turns into coal in a million years.

Though leaves rot, or leaves burn in the gutter;
though the complications of this morning's breakfast
dissolve in faint shudders of light
at a great distance, he continues to daydream
that the past is a country under the ground
where the days practice their old habits
over and over, as faint and persistent
as cigarette smoke in an airless room.
He wishes he could travel there like a tourist
and photograph the unseizable days
in the sunlight, in Connecticut, in an old chair.

❧ The Alligator Bride

The clock of my days winds down.
The cat eats sparrows outside my window.
Once, she brought me a small rabbit
which we devoured together, under
the Empire Table
while the men shrieked
repossessing the gold umbrella.

Now the beard on my clock turns white.
My cat stares into dark corners
missing her gold umbrella.
She is in love
with the Alligator Bride.

Ah, the tiny fine white
teeth! The Bride, propped on her tail
in white lace
stares from the holes
of her eyes. Her stuck-open mouth
laughs at minister and people.

On bare new wood
fourteen tomatoes,
a dozen ears of corn,
six bottles of white wine
a melon,
a cat,
broccoli
and the Alligator Bride.

The color of bubble gum,
the consistency of petroleum jelly,
wickedness oozes
from the palm of my left hand.
My cat licks it.
I watch the Alligator Bride.

Big houses like shabby boulders
hold themselves tight
in gelatin.
I am unable to daydream.
The sky is a gun aimed at me.
I pull the trigger.
The skull of my promises
leans in a black closet, gapes
with its good mouth
for a teat to suck.

A bird flies back and forth
in my house that is covered by gelatin
and the cat leaps at it
missing. Under the Empire Table
the Alligator Bride
lies in her bridal shroud.
My left hand
leaks on the Chinese carpet.

∾ Mount Kearsarge

Great blue mountain! Ghost.
I look at you
from the porch of the farmhouse
where I watched you all summer
as a boy. Steep sides, narrow flat
patch on top —
you are clear to me
like the memory of one day.
Blue! Blue!
The top of the mountain floats
in haze.
I will not rock on this porch
when I am old. I turn my back on you,
Kearsarge, I close
my eyes, and you rise inside me,
blue ghost.

❧ "Reclining Figure"

from Henry Moore's sculpture

Then the knee of the wave
turned to stone.

By the cliff of her flank
I anchored,

In the darkness of harbors
laid-by.

❦ The Town of Hill

Back of the dam, under
a flat pad

of water, church
bells ring

in the ears of lilies,
a child's swing

curls in the current
of a yard, horned

pout sleep
in a green

mailbox, and
a boy walks

from a screened
porch beneath

the man-shaped
leaves of an oak

down the street looking
at the town

of Hill that water
covered forty

years ago,
and the screen

door shuts
under dream water.

✤ Maple Syrup

August, goldenrod blowing. We walk
into the graveyard, to find
my grandfather's grave. Ten years ago
I came here last, bringing
marigolds from the round garden
outside the kitchen.
I didn't know you then.
                            We walk
among carved names that go with photographs
on top of the piano at the farm:
Keneston, Wells, Fowler, Batchelder, Buck.
We pause at the new grave
of Grace Fenton, my grandfather's
sister. Last summer
we called on her at the nursing home,
eighty-seven, and nodding
in a blue housedress. We cannot find
my grandfather's grave.
                            Back at the house
where no one lives, we potter
and explore the back chamber
where everything comes to rest: spinning wheels,
pretty boxes, quilts,
bottles, books, albums of postcards.
Then with a flashlight we descend
firm steps to the root cellar—black,
cobwebby, huge,
with dirt floors and fieldstone walls,
and above the walls, holding the hewn

sills of the house, enormous
granite foundation stones.
Past the empty bins
for squash, apples, carrots, and potatoes,
we discover the shelves for canning, a few
pale pints
of tomato left, and—what
is this?—syrup, maple syrup
in a quart jar, syrup
my grandfather made twenty-five
years ago
for the last time.
                              I remember
coming to the farm in March
in sugaring time, as a small boy.
He carried the pails of sap, sixteen-quart
buckets, dangling from each end
of a wooden yoke
that lay across his shoulders, and emptied them
into a vat in the saphouse
where fire burned day and night
for a week.
                    Now the saphouse
tilts, nearly to the ground,
like someone exhausted
to the point of death, and next winter
when snow piles three feet thick
on the roofs of the cold farm,
the saphouse will shudder and slide
with the snow to the ground.

                    Today
        we take my grandfather's last
        quart of syrup
        upstairs, holding it gingerly,
        and we wash off twenty-five years
        of dirt, and we pull
        and pry the lid up, cutting the stiff,
        dried rubber gasket, and dip our fingers
        in, you and I both, and taste
        the sweetness, you for the first time,
        the sweetness preserved, of a dead man
        in the kitchen he left
        when his body slid
        like anyone's into the ground.

◈ Ox Cart Man

In October of the year,
he counts potatoes dug from the brown field,
counting the seed, counting
the cellar's portion out,
and bags the rest on the cart's floor.

He packs wool sheared in April, honey
in combs, linen, leather
tanned from deerhide,
and vinegar in a barrel
hooped by hand at the forge's fire.

He walks by his ox's head, ten days
to Portsmouth Market, and sells potatoes,
and the bag that carried potatoes,
flaxseed, birch brooms, maple sugar, goose
feathers, yarn.

When the cart is empty he sells the cart.
When the cart is sold he sells the ox,
harness and yoke, and walks
home, his pockets heavy
with the year's coin for salt and taxes,

and at home by fire's light in November cold
stitches new harness
for next year's ox in the barn,
and carves the yoke, and saws planks
building the cart again.

⤳ Names of Horses

All winter your brute shoulders strained against collars, padding
and steerhide over the ash hames, to haul
sledges of cordwood for drying through spring and summer,
for the Glenwood stove next winter, and for the simmering
     range.

In April you pulled cartloads of manure to spread on the fields,
dark manure of Holsteins, and knobs of your own clustered with
     oats.
All summer you mowed the grass in meadow and hayfield, the
     mowing machine
clacketing beside you, while the sun walked high in the morning;

and after noon's heat, you pulled a clawed rake through the same
     acres,
gathering stacks, and dragged the wagon from stack to stack,
and the built hayrack back, uphill to the chaffy barn,
three loads of hay a day from standing grass in the morning.

Sundays you trotted the two miles to church with the light load
of a leather quartertop buggy, and grazed in the sound of hymns.
Generation on generation, your neck rubbed the windowsill
of the stall, smoothing the wood as the sea smooths glass.

When you were old and lame, when your shoulders hurt
    bending to graze,
one October the man, who fed you and kept you, and harnessed
    you every morning,
led you through corn stubble to sandy ground above Eagle Pond,
and dug a hole beside you where you stood shuddering in your
    skin,

and lay the shotgun's muzzle in the boneless hollow behind
    your ear,
and fired the slug into your brain, and felled you into your grave,
shoveling sand to cover you, setting goldenrod upright above
    you,
where by next summer a dent in the ground made your
    monument.

For a hundred and fifty years, in the pasture of dead horses,
roots of pine trees pushed through the pale curves of your ribs,
yellow blossoms flourished above you in autumn, and in winter
frost heaved your bones in the ground — old toilers, soil makers:

O Roger, Mackerel, Riley, Ned, Nellie, Chester, Lady Ghost.

❧ Merle Bascom's .22

"I was twelve when my father gave me this .22
Mossberg carbine—hand-made, with a short octagonal
barrel, stylish as an Indianfighter posing
for a photograph. We ripped up Bokar coffeecans
set into the sandbank by the track—competitive
and companionable. He was a good shot, although
his hands already trembled. Or I walked with my friend
Paul who loved airplanes and wanted to be a pilot,
and carried my rifle loosely, pointing it downward;
I aimed at squirrels and missed. Later I shot woodchucks
that ate my widowed mother's peas and Kentucky
Wonders when I visited on weekends from college,
or drove up from my Boston suburb, finding the gun
in its closet behind the woodstove. Ten years ago
my mother died; I sold up, and moved here with my work
and my second wife, gladly taking my tenancy
in the farmhouse where I intended to live and die.
I used my rifle on another generation
of woodchucks that ate our beans. One autumn an old friend
from college stayed with us after a nervous breakdown:
trembling from electroshock, depressed, suicidal.
I wrapped the octagonal Mossberg in a burlap
bag and concealed it under boards in the old grainshed.
In our quiet house he strengthened and stopped shaking.
When he went home I neglected to retrieve my gun,
and the next summer woodchucks took over the garden.
I let them. Our lives fitted mountain, creek, and hayfield.
Long days like minnows in the pond quickened and were still.
When I looked up from Plutarch another year had passed.

One Sunday the choir at our church sang Whittier's hymn
ending with 'the still small voice of calm.' Idly I thought,
'I must ask them to sing that hymn at my funeral.'
Soon after, I looked for the .22 in the shed,
half expecting it to have vanished, but finding it
wrapped intact where I left it, hardly rusted. I spent
a long evening taking it apart and cleaning it;
I thought of my father's hands shaking as he aimed it.
Then I restored the Mossberg to its accustomed place
in the closet behind the stove. At about this time
I learned that my daughter-in-law was two months pregnant:
It would be the first grandchild. One day I was walking
alone and imagined a granddaughter visiting:
She loved the old place; she swam in the summer pond
     with us;
she walked with us in red October; she grew older, she fell
in love with a neighbor, she married . . . As I daydreamed,
suddenly I was seized by a fit of revulsion:
I thought: 'Must I go through all that again? Must I live
another twenty years?' It was as if a body
rose from a hole where I had buried it years ago
while my first marriage was twisting and thrashing to death.
One night I was drunk and lost control of my Beetle
off 128 near my ranchhouse. I missed a curve
at seventy miles an hour and careened toward a stone wall.
In a hundredth of a second I knew I would die;
and, as joy fired through my body, I knew something else.
But the car slowed itself on rocks and settled to rest
between an elm and a maple; I sat breathing,
feeling the joy leach out, leaving behind the torment
and terror of my desire. Now I felt this affliction
descend again and metastasize through my body.

Today I drove ninety miles, slowly, seatbelt fastened,
to North Andover and Paul's house, where he lives flying
out of Logan for United. I asked him to hide
the firing pin on an octagonal .22.
He nodded and took it from my hands without speaking.
I cannot throw it away; it was my father's gift."

❦ The Day I Was Older

The Clock
The clock on the parlor wall, stout as a mariner's clock,
disperses the day. All night it tolls the half-hour
and the hour's number with resolute measure,
approaching the poles and crossing the equator
over fathoms of sleep. Warm
in the dark next to your breathing,
below the thousand favored stars, I feel
horns of gray water heave
underneath us, and the ship's pistons
pound as the voyage continues over the limited sea.

The News
After tending the fire, making coffee, and pouring milk
for cats, I sit in a blue chair each morning,
reading obituaries in the *Boston Globe*
for the mean age: today there is MANUFACTURER CONCORD 53,
EX-CONGRESSMAN SAUGUS 80 — and I read
that Emily Farr is dead, after a long illness in Oregon.
Once in an old house we talked for an hour, while a coalfire
brightened in November twilight and wavered
our shadows high on the wall
until our eyes fixed on each other. Thirty years ago.

The Pond
We lie by the pond on a late August afternoon
as a breeze from low hills in the west stiffens water
and agitates birch leaves yellowing above us.
You set down your book
and lift your eyes to white trunks tilting from shore.
A mink scuds through ferns; an acorn tumbles.
Soon we will turn to our daily business.
You do not know that I am watching, taking pleasure
in your breasts that rise and fall as you breathe.
Then I see mourners gathered by an open grave.

The Day
Last night at suppertime I outlived my father, enduring
the year, month, day, and hour
when he lay back on a hospital bed in the guestroom
among cylinders of oxygen — mouth open, nostrils and lips
fixed unquivering, pale blue. Now I have wakened
more mornings to frost whitening the grass,
read the newspaper more times, and stood more times,
my hand on the doorknob without opening the door.
Father of my name, father of long fingers, I remember
your dark hair, and your face almost unwrinkled.

The Cup
From the Studebaker's backseat, on our Sunday drives,
I watched her earrings sway. Then I walked uphill
beside an old man carrying buckets
under birches on an August day. Striding at noontime,
I looked at wheat and at river cities. I kissed the cheek
of my father dying. By the pond an acorn fell.
You listening here, you reading these words as I write them,
I offer this cup to you: Though we drink
from this cup every day, we will never drink it dry.

∽⅋∾ Prophecy

I will strike down wooden houses; I will burn aluminum
clapboard skin; I will strike down garages
where crimson Toyotas sleep side by side; I will explode
palaces of gold, silver, and alabaster:—the summer
great house and its folly together. Where shopping malls
spread plywood and plaster out, and roadhouses
serve steak and potatoskins beside Alaska king crab;
where triangular flags proclaim tribes of identical campers;
where airplanes nose to tail exhale kerosene,
weeds and ashes will drowse in continual twilight.

I reject the old house and the new car; I reject
Tory and Whig together; I reject the argument
that modesty of ambition is sensible because the bigger
they are the harder they fall; I reject Waterford;
I reject the five and dime; I reject Romulus and Remus;
I reject Martha's Vineyard and the slamdunk contest;
I reject leaded panes; I reject the appointment made
at the tennis net or on the seventeenth green; I reject
the Professional Bowlers Tour; I reject matchboxes;
I reject purple bathrooms with purple soap in them.

Men who lie awake worrying about taxes, vomiting
at dawn, whose hands shake as they administer Valium, —
skin will peel from the meat of their thighs.
Armies that march all day with elephants past pyramids
and roll pulling missiles past generals weary of saluting
and past president-emperors splendid in cloth-of-gold, —
soft rumps of armies will dissipate in rain. Where square
miles of corn waver in Minnesota, where tobacco ripens
in Carolina and apples in New Hampshire, where wheat
turns Kansas green, where pulpmills stink Oregon, —

dust will blow in the darkness and cactus die
before it flowers. Where skiers wait for chairlifts,
wearing money, low raspberries will part rib bones.
Where the drive-in church raises a chromium cross,
dandelions and milkweed will straggle through blacktop.
I will strike from the ocean with waves afire;
I will strike from the hill with rainclouds of lava;
I will strike from darkened air
with melanoma in the shape of decorative hexagonals.
I will strike down embezzlers and eaters of snails.

I reject Japanese smoked oysters, potted chrysanthemums
allowed to die, Tupperware parties, Ronald McDonald,
Kaposi's sarcoma, the Taj Mahal, Holsteins wearing
electronic necklaces, the Algonquin, Tunisian aqueducts,
Phi Beta Kappa keys, the Hyatt Embarcadero, carpenters
jogging on the median, and betrayal that engorges
the corrupt heart longing for criminal surrender.
I reject shadows in the corner of the atrium
where Phyllis or Phoebe speaks with Billy or Marc
who says that afternoons are best although not reliable.

Your children will wander looting the shopping malls
for forty years, suffering for your idleness,
until the last dwarf body rots in a parking lot.
I will strike down lobbies and restaruants in motels
carpeted with shaggy petrochemicals
from Maine to Hilton Head, from the Skagit to Tucson.
I will strike down hang gliders, wiry adventurous boys;
their thigh bones will snap, their brains
slide from their skulls. I will strike down
families cooking wildboar in New Mexico backyards.

Then landscape will clutter with incapable machinery,
acres of vacant airplanes and schoolbuses, ploughs
with seedlings sprouting and turning brown through colters.
Unlettered dwarves will burrow for warmth and shelter
in the caves of dynamos and Plymouths, dying
of old age at seventeen. Tribes wandering
in the wilderness of their ignorant desolation,
who suffer from your idleness, will burn your illuminated
missals to warm their rickety bodies.
Terrorists assemble plutonium because you are idle

and industrious. The whip-poor-will shrivels
and the pickerel chokes under the government of self-love.
Vacancy burns air so that you strangle without oxygen
like rats in a biologist's bell jar. The living god sharpens
the scythe of my prophecy to strike down red poppies
and blue cornflowers. When priests and policemen
strike my body's match, Jehovah will flame out;
Jehovah will suck air from the vents of bombshelters.
Therefore let the Buick swell until it explodes;
therefore let anorexia starve and bulimia engorge.

When Elzira leaves the house wearing her tennis dress
and drives her black Porsche to meet Abraham,
quarrels, returns to husband and children, and sobs
asleep, drunk, unable to choose among them, —
lawns and carpets will turn into tar together
with lovers, husbands, and children.
Fat will boil in the sacs of children's clear skin.
I will strike down the nations, astronauts and judges;
I will strike down Babylon, I will strike acrobats,
I will strike algae and the white birches.

Because professors of law teach ethics in dumbshow,
let the colonel become president; because chief executive
officers and commissars collect down for pillows,
let the injustice of cities burn city and suburb;
let the countryside burn; let the pineforests of Maine
explode like a kitchenmatch and the Book of Kells turn
ash in a microsecond; let oxen and athletes
flash into grease: — I return to Appalachian rocks;
I shall eat bread; I shall prophesy through millennia
of Jehovah's day until the sky reddens over cities:

The houses will burn, even houses of alabaster;
the sky will disappear like a scroll rolled up
and hidden in a cave from the industries of idleness.
Mountains will erupt and vanish, becoming deserts,
and the sea wash over the sea's lost islands
and the earth split open like a corpse's gassy
stomach and the sun turn as black as a widow's skirt
and the full moon grow red with blood swollen inside it
and stars fall from the sky like wind-blown apples, —
while Babylon's managers burn in the rage of the Lamb.

AN INTERVIEW
WITH
DONALD HALL

AN INTERVIEW WITH DONALD HALL

⤸   Liam Rector   ⤸

LIAM RECTOR: You've written poignantly about time and generations. Jose Ortega y Gasset had a scheme for generation:

Ages:	1 to 15	Childhood
	15 to 30	Youth
	30 to 45	Initiation
	45 to 60	Dominance
	60 to 75	Old Age, "Outside of Life"

How have these moments moved in consort with the time of your life, your work, and the scheme of literary generations as you've experienced them?

DONALD HALL: Schemes irritate me. Maybe this scheme annoys me because I'm supposed to move "outside of life" in a few months and I'm damned if I'm ready to. Rigidities, separations get my back up. Maybe I left childhood at fourteen and remained adolescent until forty-three. I like the word "dominance"—and I suppose I felt it first about fifty, though I think I was looking for it from the age of fifteen. So I respond, not by generality on the schemer's level, but autobiographically or egotistically. Chronological skeletons—like somatic or psychological types, like classes, like historical determinism: hell, like the goddamned horoscope!—provide things to talk about, frameworks for discussion . . . But if you accept them, and

Reprinted from *The American Poetry Review,* by permission of the editor. Copyright © 1989 Liam Rector.

not rebel against them, you actively desire the comfort of prison! Everything's done for you; relax: prison . . . or *tenure*.

RECTOR: In the essay, "Rusticus," you said you grew up in Hamden, Connecticut, a suburb of New Haven, in a "massclass' neighborhood wherein everyone more or less shared four convictions: "1) I will do better than my father and mother. 2) My children will do better than I do. 3) 'Better' includes 'education,' and education provides the things of this world. 4) *The things of this world are good.*" *String Too Short to Be Saved* speaks powerfully for the summer life in New Hampshire you experienced as a boy, but could you say more about the culture and class in which you grew up in Hamden? *Have* you done better?

HALL: In the suburban neighborhood where I grew up in Connecticut, the houses were like each other; the cars that belonged to the houses resembled each other; the fathers, working at their different jobs, had incomes roughly similar; the mothers weren't supposed to work, and their leisure or volunteer-work decorated the fathers. In school, there were rewards for conformity and punishments for difference. In the culture of the country, where I spent my summers, there was fantastic diversity — in education, aspiration, income, appearance; what you wore, what you ate, what you did for fun: from house to house along the roads and lanes. Eccentricity was a *value*; a major ethical notion was everybody's right to be different. I belonged to the Connecticut culture and longed for the other. I live in the other now — it's not greatly changed — and live by it, observe it, write about it — but of course I will never be truly *of* it. My whole life comes out of the conflict of these cultures — and my choice to love and inhabit the one rather than the other.

RECTOR: You went to the Phillips Exeter Academy and then to Harvard, Oxford, and Stanford. Did the students at these schools share the cultural and class background you outlined in the essay "Rusticus"? You then went on to the public, sprawling world of the University of Michigan to teach. What led you to attend these schools as a student, and what went into the decision to teach at Michigan?

HALL: The class structure in England is unlike ours, and I won't try to describe it. Sure, other students at Exeter were mostly from the same suburbs, where people try to resemble each other, but most came from more money than I did. My parents sent me there because they knew it was a good school, I don't think for social reasons at all. They weren't social people. At Exeter the best teachers all came from Harvard; the best students were going there — quickly I knew I wanted to go there. Some Exeter kids came from money that had been around in the family longer. At Harvard I felt less of this: There was more diversity there, at least among the people I knew. Even at that time Harvard was more high school than prep school, trying to get the best high school students from all over the country. They were a bunch of tigers locked in a small cage; I liked that. I tried for a fellowship to Oxford because it was a plum and because it sounded like fun to travel an live in another country. While I was there England was in a bad way economically. I never saw my English friends on the continent during holiday because they were only allowed to take twenty-five pounds out of the country in a year. There were already lots of scholarship boys at Oxford, but I was so separate culturally — older, from another nation. Being an outsider gave me privileges which I enjoyed, privileges to be weird.

One of the reasons I went to the University of Michigan was to get away from the Harvard which I liked so much. After I did the B.A. I spent only three years away at first — Oxford and Stanford — then returned for three more years in the Society of Fellows. There were pathetic sorts around the Square who would take any sort of rotten job in order not to leave Cambridge, or — perish the thought! — go to the *Middle West*. (America's geographical snobbery is repulsive.) I wanted to get away, to try another kind of institution, and Michigan made a good offer. Ironically — probably predictably! — I went to an institution which, within Michigan and nearby states, is considered rather snobbish, rather old school tie. Some students' grandparents and parents had belonged to the same fraternities and sororities — but there were children of lineworkers. I liked that variety, that looseness.

RECTOR: We both grew up spending our summers with our grandparents on farms, you in New Hampshire and I in Virginia. In *String* you wrote of how this shaped your imagination and that residence where imagination and memory comingle. Living now on that same farm where you spent summers, what is your memory, your imagination of the large cities?

HALL: I've never lived in a great city. For me, large cities are excitement, energy, vitality, almost mania. When I go to New York I never sleep. Oh, I've lived for a month or two at a time in London, Paris, Rome. Because Cambridge is virtually Boston, and I went to school there, I suppose I *did* live in a big city — but living in a college isn't the same. I contrast the country not to the city but to the suburbs; Ann Arbor is a suburb without an urb. (Technically it's a city.)

This place is no longer a farm but the rural culture remains amazingly intact, although thirty years ago I thought it was vanishing. I love the landscape more deeply all the time; I am content sitting on the porch and gazing at Kearsarge; or walking in the woods. Carol Bly speaks somewhere of writers who are "mindless nature describers." Touché; I guess I'm a mindless nature lover, but I love also the independence and solitude of the country, which is by no means only a matter of population density. I don't suffer from the deference, mostly ironic, that hangs around writers in universities; I'm the "fellow over there who writes books for a living" and that's a freedom.

RECTOR: Your work has been haunted not only by the grandfather but the father. Did your father encourage you to become a writer?

HALL: My father was soft and volatile, a businessman who hated being a businessman and daydreamed for himself a life in the academy — probably prep school rather than college — where everybody would be *kind* to everybody else. He read books; mostly he read contemporary historical fiction like Hervey Allen and Kenneth Roberts. He was finicky about good prose and suffered from polysyllabic tendencies, especially if he was depressed: "It is necessary to masticate thoroughly." Politically he was conservative and not very thoughful. He wept frequently and showed feelings which other men would hold back. He desperately wanted people to like him and many did. He was nervous, continually shaking; quick, alert, sensitive, unintellectual. When he was forty-two he hemorrhaged with a bad bleeding ulcer and remained sickly until he got lung cancer at fifty-one and died at fifty-two. As an adolescent I needed to feel superior to him; when I was about twenty-five, when my son was born, I felt reconciled. I don't think we talked about matters of great substance but we could love each other. He read my things and mostly praised them, but I don't think either of us wanted to talk about them. He tried to encourage me in one direction, constantly, by telling me that my poetry was just fine but my prose was really great. . . . Some of this at least was his desire that I might possibly be able to make a living. When he realized that I was going into teaching, it pleased him because of his imaginary academy.

RECTOR: Your new book, *The One Day*, is in many ways a departure from *Kicking the Leaves* and *The Happy Man*, both in its elliptical form, its being a book-length shoring of fragments, and its engagement with the very old and the very new, aside from your personal remembered past which sets much of the tone in the two books before. How do you account for this shift? One section of *The One Day*, "Shrubs Burnt Away," was printed in *The Happy Man*. What made you decide to foreshadow the long poem by printing it there? Had you yet seen the shape that *The One Day* would assume?

HALL: If you look at everything from the beginning in 1955, there is lots of moving about and shifting. Surely you're right that the form of *The One Day* is Modernist, with its multiple protagonist—but I guess I don't want to. . . . Really, I don't want to talk about the form of it. It's new; I'm still finding out what I did.

The poem began with an onslaught of language back in 1971. Over a period of weeks I kept receiving messages; I filled page after page of notebooks. If I drove to the supermarket, I had to bring the book and pull over three or four times in a few miles to transcribe what was coming. It was inchoate, sloppy, but full of *material*: verbal, imaginative, recollected. And it was frightening. After a while the barrage ceased, but from time to time over the years more would come—with a little label on it, telling me that it belonged to this *thing*. (In my head for a long time I called it *Building the House of Dying*.) The first part was there in inchoate form, much of the first two of "Four Classic Texts," much of the "one day" theme in the third part. Every now and then, over the years, I would look at these notebooks, and feel excitement and fear. In 1980 I began to *work* on it; to try to do something with these words. First I set it out as a series of twenty-five or thirty linked free verse poems: Nothing marched. I worked on it for a year or two; I remember reading it aloud to Jane one time, and when I finished I was full of *shame!* Shame over what I revealed, shame over bad poetry; after that, I couldn't look at it for a year.

At some point early in the 1980s, Robert Mazzocco suggested casually in a letter that I ought sometime to write a book of linked poems, like Lowell in *Notebook* or Berryman in *Dream Songs*. Thinking of this notion I developed my ten-line stanza, making some into almost-discrete ten-line poems, using others as stanzas. I thought of Keats's *Ode* stanza, developed out of the sonnet and the desire to write the longer ode-form. This notion helped me get to work: bricks—cement blocks?—for the house. I worked with these stanzas for a couple of years, then maybe in 1984 developed a three-part idea that *somewhat* resembles the present version, except that the middle part is totally different. I showed a draft to a few people. I remember Bly saying, with his usual diffidence, that the first part was the best thing I had ever done. The second part was a problem until I worked out the notion that turned into "Four Classic Texts;" I stole "Eclogue" from Virgil, which always helps. I still thought the third part was my real problem, and sometimes doubted that I would ever finish the whole — because I wouldn't be able to make the third part.

When I put *The Happy Man* together I had "Shrubs Burnt Away" more or less finished, "Four Classic Texts" just beginning, and "In the One Day" lying about in pieces. I thought it would be ten years before I would be able to finish the poem as a whole, if I ever did. I had no notion that I might finish it within a couple of years. But I think that printing "Shrubs" in *The Happy Man* allowed me to finish the whole poem. Response was encouraging . . . and some reviews helped me understand what I was doing, like David Shapiro's in *Poetry*, with his reference to Freud and the movement from hysterical misery to ordinary unhappiness!

RECTOR: What about your work in children's books?

HALL: I've worked on children's books for twenty-five years, starting when Andrew was a little boy, and I've written many — but only published four. The first was *Andrew the Lion Farmer*, which I may rewrite and reissue. That one came out of storytelling with Andrew when he was four years old. I made up lots of stories. Then one day he said he had a great, scary idea: He was going to go to the lion store and buy a lion seed and grow a lion from a pot! . . . Wow! I was *off!* Now I don't have four year olds around anymore — maybe I'll make up stories for grandchildren one day — but there's a permanent four-year-old in my head, to whom I tell my stories. I've worked on three in the last year, but none is any good. If you have the proper shape, the *fable*, maybe they're not so hard to write — economy, limits of diction, right details . . . But finding the fable is hard! For each of my juveniles, the publishers found the illustrator, asking my approval; then the illustrator has asked me questions, maybe shown me samples. I've been fortunate: Barbara Cooney, Mary Azarian.

RECTOR: Does the war of the anthologies (yours, Pack's, and Simpson's vs. the Donald Allen anthology) stay with you to this day? (Even though you included the work of Ginsberg, Snyder, and others in a later anthology you edited for Penguin?) What young turks have you lived to see become old deacons?

HALL: The war of the anthologies was real enough, back at the end of the fifties. For some nostalgic and sentimental people it still goes on; ah, the barricades! They remind me of people in my parents' generation, who lived out their lives in nostalgia over Prohibition. Bathtub gin! Speakeasies! . . . I speak without disinterest, because I am still loathed here and there as a leader of the Eastern Establishment, Mr. Hallpack Simpson, Enemy, Archbishop of Academic Poetry! . . . People want to relive their youths, when good was good and bad was stanzas.

For the most part good poets want no part of it. Creeley and I, Ginsberg and I, were famous enemies . . . but we stopped twenty-five years ago. In 1961 Denise Levertov, who was poetry editor at *The Nation*, asked me to review Charles Olson's first *The Maximus Poems*. Ecumenism was already there. In 1962 I did my Penguin with Levertov, Creeley, and Snyder, only five years after Hallpack. (Five years is a long time when it starts in your twenties.) By 1961 I was abashed by the rigidity that defended my citadel when I was in my mid-twenties.

I don't think that *particular* war endures except for nostalgic diehards—but there will always be outs and ins; and the first shall be last: sometimes. I see geographical complacency and enmity now. What is a Los Angeles poem? (I don't think there's a New Hampshire poem.) For the most part, geographical groups are diffident folk trying to build castles to feel safe in. To hell with it. I want to be a poet by myself, not a New England poet or a deep image poet or what have you. In my own generation in America, the poet I admire the most is not considered a member of my gang. Robert Creeley.

RECTOR: Those anthologies provided a dialectic for their time. Does such a dialectic exist now, or is it a time of synthesis, revision, mannerism, or utter impasse? Was the aesthetic distance between your and Allen's anthology a real one? Are you ever tempted to edit another anthology of younger poets, at your age?

HALL: I've been asked to edit an anthology of the young and I have refused. Let the young edit the young. I could do it — but the passion would not be there, and if I made fewer gross mistakes the whole thing would be a big mistake. I don't like recent anthologies of younger poets because they are too damned big. Out of generosity or whatever, probably whatever, they include too many aspirants and contribute to the confusion of numbers.

I don't really think there's a dialectic now though it seems so to some. Metrical poets against the world. Free-verse plain-talk poets against the world. Language Poets against the world. Narrative poets against the world. There's a comfort in being *out*, and people warm themselves by that cold fire. But conflict *does* make energy. Maybe it's a time of warring tribes, Balkanization, rather than a time of dueling superpowers. Oh, it wasn't really superpowers ever, not even back then . . . Allen Ginsberg, Frank O'Hara, Robert Duncan, Denise Levertov, and John Ashbery did not resemble each other.

RECTOR: What's good about growing older?

HALL: What's bad about growing older is the knowledge that you have less *time*, the frustration that you will not live to write the books or the poems; or to read all the books you want to. What is good, paradoxically enough, is patience. With less time I feel or act as if I had more. When I begin a poem of any ambition, I know that I will be working on it five years from now; I *sigh* a little . . . but I get on with it. I feel more energy, need less sleep, feel more excitement about work than I did when I was thirty or forty. I've been lucky in my second marriage, in living where I want to live; these are not inevitable results of aging.

RECTOR: Simpson says he has scolded you for writing so much about the business of poetry — the number of books sold, number of readings, etc. What do you think about that? (Rexroth also wrote of these matters, yes?)

HALL: Louis and I fight about lots of things. He was outraged when I wrote an article about poetry readings. I write essays in poetic theory, and essays of appreciation, but from time to time I write essays of fact. I am interested, for example, in how writers make their livings; I always liked *New Grub Street*, and biographies. Think of Emerson making his living by traveling around the country, at first by steamer and stagecoach, lecturing week after week — like Robert Bly. It annoys me that people generalize, as if facts were common knowledge, when they don't know the facts. One constantly hears how poetry sells less than it ever did; even publishers say so; and the numbers are different. The *facts* don't necessarily have anything to do with quality — I grant Louis that — but let's find out the facts before we generalize. If poets typically make a living as teachers, is their workday unrelated to the poetry that they write? I used to be fascinated by all the English poets who lived by their wits free-lancing. A couple of centuries ago a good many were vicars. The poetry reading must explain a great deal — good and bad — about the kind of poetry that is written today. There is also the phenomenon of the creative writing industry.

RECTOR: What do you think accounts for the dearth of polemics in current writings about poetics? Compared to Pound and Lewis's *Blast*, Bly's *The Fifties*, why do we see so few picking up the cudgel these days? Is it part of an "I'm okay; you're okay" relativism and "Make Nice" culture, or just a period of exhaustion, politeness, or fear?

HALL: Compare the reviews in English magazines! Nastiness is a dumb convention over there as our namby-pambyness is a dumb convention here. "Boost Don't Knock," said the Boosters Club. How many poets have you heard say that they don't want to review anything unless they can praise it? Oh, I don't believe in taking a cannon to kill a flea. It's a waste of time to write a savage review of a book that nobody is going to read. But I believe in taking a cannon to kill a flea continually described as an eagle. I've tried to do it once or twice.

RECTOR: What do you think about creative writing programs being separated from English departments and being put under the aegis, say, of a Fine Arts department, along with dancers, musicians, theater people?

HALL: Separating creative writing from the regular English department is a disaster. "Here are the people who can read; here are the people who can write. People who can write can't read; people who can read can't write." Wonderful. Specialization is a curse, especially for poets. Separate departments divide old poetry from new. Some places have literature departments *within* creative writing departments, where writers teach reading to would-be writers. But the value of writers to English departments lies not in teaching of creative writing; it's their teaching of literature classes for regular undergraduates or graduates. Of course most Ph.D.s are dopes; so are most poets. Undergraduate English majors — or engineers and nurses taking an elective — suffer because they never get to be taught by a writer. The faculty suffers because separations make for complacency; nobody's challenging you with an alternative; but the teacher of creative writing suffers most. When you teach literature you spend your days with great work — reading it, talking about it, reading papers about it. Great literature rubs off and you *learn* by teaching, by encountering what you don't know well enough, teaching it to people who know it even less. This separation makes for narcissism, complacency, and ignorance: it's the worst thing that has happened with the creative writing industry. People spend whole lives talking about line-breaks and *The New Yorker!*

RECTOR: You've said that poets should be teaching literature rather than conducting writing workshops. Why?

HALL: If you teach great literature you live among the great models. You make you living reading Moore and Pound and Hardy and Marvell and Yeats! Incredible. Students ask you questions, and when you answer you discover that you knew something you didn't know you knew. Instead of living with half-baked first drafts by narcissistic teenagers, you live with the *greatest art.* What could be a better way to spend your spare time — when you're not competing directly with Wordsworth — than by reading Wordsworth?

RECTOR: The first readers for your poems — Bly, Kinnell, Simpson, Bidart, Orr, and others . . . How have their readings changed and developed over time?

HALL: Jane Kenyon is my first reader and has been for fifteen years. Robert Bly has read virtually every poem I've written for forty years. Simpson, Snodgrass, Kinnell . . . These people have helped me enormously through the years. For a while in our twenties Adrienne Rich and I worked on each other's poems. When we lived near each other, Gregory Orr helped me. I haven't known Frank Bidart so long but he has been extremely helpful; Robert Pinsky on occasion, Wendell Berry very often. Bly's reading has changed the most. He used to cut and rewrite; sometimes I took his corrections and put them in print: More often they showed me what was wrong and helped me make my own changes. More recently he has taken to speaking more about the underneath of the poem, touching the text less. Galway is a marvelous editor, a great cutter. Snodgrass is superb at a Johnsonian reading, following syntax and implication, allowing himself to be puzzled.

RECTOR: What goes into your choosing someone to be such a reader of your work? Their ability to argue their position? You said in an *Iowa Review* interview with David Hamilton that the criticism of younger writers has not been of much use to you. Why is that?

HALL: I don't choose anybody. We choose each other — a mating dance, tentative advances and retreats. Criticism *must* be mutual, a dialogue. It doesn't work when criticism goes in one direction only. And the poetics has to have something in common; if two people are simply opposed, there's no common ground where conversation can happen. And it helps to get your own notions thrown back at you when you violate them. Within a general agreement, then you should be as different as possible—like Bly and me.

The requirements are more temperamental than generational. Since that interview with David Hamilton, I have made great use of some young readers. (Young compared to me.) With some young poets, you sense that they may be frightened, or deferential, or counter-deferential which is just as bad—acting nastier than they feel, in order to show that they're not cowed. When I answered Hamilton, I was thinking of some dreadful examples of young fans praising elderly slop; the young were sincere but dazzled. I don't forgive the old for believing what they want to believe.

RECTOR: You're one of the few writers your age I know who still reads and comments on the work of younger writers, aside from people who formally teach or are busy writing blurbs. Most writers, once they reach fifty or so, confine themselves to reading the work of their own generation and work of the distant past? Why has this been different for you?

HALL: I keep looking. I'm *curious:* What's happening? What's going to happen? I've seen nothing so extraordinary as the increased *numbers* of poets, people with at least some ability; the numbers especially of young women, compared to earlier generations, including mine. Because I was so rigid when I was young, I try to stay open to kinds of poetry alien to my own; of course openness can become a mindless relativism or namby-pambyness. You have to worry: Do I just want them to *like* me? One thing I learned ten or twenty years ago: If you read something that upsets you, that violates every canon you ever considered . . . look again, look harder: It might be *poetry*. This notion helped me read Frank Bidart. I read the Language Poets without great success, but some please me more than others: Perelman, Palmer, Hejinian, Silliman.

You can't keep up forever. I look into as many as six hundred new books a year. I'm not telling you that I read every poem; I get tired. Like everybody else I get tired reading the same poem over and over again, but it's not only that. When I was in my twenties Richard Eberhart, who was only fifty, told me that he could no longer tell the young apart. He was not being insulting; he was complaining, not bragging. I suppose it happens to everyone. Maybe it begins to happen to me; but I remain avid to *keep up*. I suppose the feeling is more acquisitive than altruistic but from time to time I can help someone. On the other hand, I continually get booklength manuscripts by mail from strangers, usually wanting me to find them a publisher. I cannot even read them all. Too much!

RECTOR: Could you speak a bit about your processes of revision?

HALL: I'm not quick. So many things have looked good and in retrospect were awful! I need to keep things around a long time; if I keep staring, I find out what's wrong. Or I think I do. Usually it takes years of staring, until I take them inside me; sometimes I wake up at night with a problem about a poem, or a solution to a problem, when I have not seen the poem for a year or more. Mostly I work on poems every day for months; then I get fed up and put them away; then I find myself obsessing about them again and drag them out and get to work.

The first twenty drafts, the poem changes rapidly — major changes, bit cuts, new directions, additions. Eventually, the last fifty drafts are small but crucial things. Oh, sometimes after three years work there's a flurry of major changes. Every poem is different.

I must say: I enjoy revising! It's the good work. The initial inspiration is over quickly, scary and manic; then I love the daily work, the struggle with language and the sweet difficulty of that struggle!

RECTOR: Your work as an editor for *The Harvard Advocate*, *The Paris Review*, the Wesleyan poetry series, Harper and Row, the University of Michigan series, and *Harvard Magazine* — how has this affected your life? What advice might you have for editors, for a long life spent tending to the work of other poets?

HALL: When you edit you impose your own taste. Especially when I was younger and passionate about the work of my own generation, I wanted to impose my taste on *everybody*. Of course at this point I no longer agree with my old taste; but I don't disavow the motive. Others editors worked with a counter-taste. Conflict makes energy, and I'm all for it. I started the Poets on Poetry series with the University of Michigan Press because I wanted to be able to read the books. I'd read an article here and there by this poet or that, but when I wanted to lay my hands on an essay I couldn't find it. I made the series in order to preserve fugitive and miscellaneous pieces — interviews, book reviews, full dress articles, what have you.

Advice: Never edit by committee! Advocate, disparage, make public what you love and what you hate! When you stop loving and hating, stop editing.

RECTOR: The Michigan Series, Poets on Poetry — Robert Mc-Dowell said in a review of the series that "The Mum

Was Always Talking." I have the suspicion, along with Mc-Dowell, that if this series were not done we would have precious little record of the poetics of your generation. Did growing up, coming to fruition in the shadow of the New Critics inhibit poets from writing prose about their poetry, from writing any kind of criticism at all? W. S. Merwin once said it had that effect on him . . .

HALL: Yes, many of us felt the way Merwin speaks. You had a feeling that some older poets would *rather* write an essay than a poem! And we reacted. Now there's a further reaction, parallel to and symptomatic of the separation of the English department from creative writing, which says that if you think about poetry—or utter thoughts about it, or allude to any poet born before 1925—you're a pedant. Bah!

RECTOR: How long did you write textbooks before you could count on any royalties from them as a basis for your income as a freelance writer?

HALL: When I quit teaching I had no confidence that my income was great enough to support my family, with my children going to college. At that time *Writing Well* made more money for me than any other book but I couldn't count on it. Really, it hasn't been textbooks that have supported us. My income derives from such a variety of sources—textbooks, juveniles, trade books—many old things bring in a pittance every year: poetry readings, magazine sales . . . *Writing Well* doesn't sell so well as it used to; other textbooks help but I don't rely on them. The many sources do a couple of things: They provide extraordinary variety in the work I do; and they have the virtues of a multiple conglomerate: if one sort of writing dwindles—

if I lose interest or the market crumbles or my ability diminishes within a genre—there's something else to pick it up. Of course these advantages are accidental; I didn't become so various on purpose. I always take pleasure in trying something new.

RECTOR: Bly looks at the world as a Jungian and you as a Freudian? How has Freud affected your view of things? What have the insights of psychology, and psycholanalysis in particular, meant to you and your generation of poets?

HALL: I started reading Freud in 1953. Ten years later I started psychotherapy with a Freudian analyst, the only analyst in Ann Arbor who would do therapy. Reading Freud was exciting and gave me ideas; I could have found much the same in Heraclitus: Whenever somebody shows you north, suspect south. Later, the experience of therapy was profound. It touches me every day and it goes *with* poetry rather than against it. You learn to release, to allow the ants—and the butterflies—to come out from under the rock; but first you have to know the rock's there! The names of the things that run out are up to you. Psychotherapy properly is never a matter of the explanations of feelings, nor of "Eureka!" as in Hollywood. It is a transforming thing. It makes your skin alert; it builds a system of sensors. Jung, on the other hand, seems a mildly interesting literary figure, full of fascinating ideas and disgusting ones mixed together with more regard for color than for truth. Freud is as nasty as the world is, as human life is. Jung is decorative. Freud is the streets and Jung is a Fourth of July parade through the streets, a parade of minor deities escaped from the zoo of polytheism. Freud has the relentlessness of monotheism.

RECTOR: Will you ever write an autobiography of your adult life?

HALL: No.

RECTOR: How do you work up a biography?

HALL: You work on a biography by interviewing everybody and reading everything and taking notes and keeping files and taking a deep breath and plunging in. Of course biography is fiction. Again and again you have to make choices because your information contradicts itself. Did it happen this way or that way? Hell, you have to make the same choices writing out of your own life! You remember something with perfect clarity and you're perfectly wrong. How can we expect that biography be true? Mind you, it is not the same as writing a novel; there are *certain* scruples.

RECTOR: You came to Whitman in your middle age? Some came to him early and take his words as scripture (I think of Ginsberg and Kinnell, particularly, here) and others arrived at him later, such as yourself and Richard Howard. What do you think might account for this?

HALL: It was my good fortune that I delayed Whitman, but as so often the provenance of the good fortune was dumb. I grew up reading poems the new critical way, which worked for Donne, and Hart Crane, but didn't work for Whitman. When I tried reading him he looked silly. My inadequacy saved him for me. He was brand new and exciting when I found him in middle age—by which I mean thirty or thirty-two.

RECTOR: Who, aside from writers, have been your most important teachers?

HALL: Henry Moore. I spent a good deal of time with him, talking with him, watching him work. He had the most wonderful attitude toward work and his art. He was interested only in being better than Michelangelo, and he knew he never achieved it; so he got up the next morning and tried again. He was a gregarious man who learned to forego companionship for the sake of work. He knew what he had to do. He remained decent to others, although it is difficult; people make it difficult for you when you're that damned famous. He knew the difference between putting in time — you can work sixteen hours a day and remain lazy — and really working as an artist, trying to *break through.*

RECTOR: How would you place your poems among the poems of the past? I'm thinking here of Keat's statement, which you mentioned in "Poetry and Ambition," that "I would sooner fail, than not be among the greatest." You've also wisely said that we are bad at judging our own work — we either think too much of it or too little of it? But take a crack at it?

HALL: I can't place my poems among the poems of the past and I doubt the sanity or the intelligence of people who say that they can. When Keats said that he would "sooner fail than not be among the greatest," note that he did not tell us that he *was* among the greatest. He *wishes* to be among the English poets when he is dead; he does not tell us that he already *is.* When I was young I had the illusion that at some point or other you would *know* if you were good. I no longer believe that such knowledge is possible. Some days you feel you're terrific; some days you feel that you're crap. So what? Get on with it.

RECTOR: You have said that during the time *The Alligator Bride* and *The Town of Hill* were published, you were floundering as a writer, conscious that nothing you did was as good as some earlier poems. Why did you publish the poems of that period?

HALL: It was from 1969 to 1975 that I floundered; *The Alligator Bride* came out in 1969 and included "The Man in the Dead Machine" which I thought (and still think) was as good as anything I had done up to then. Also I liked the title poem and several other new things — but after *The Alligator*, for six years, I felt that nothing that I was doing was as good as what I had done. I didn't think that what I was writing was beneath contempt; it's melancholy enough to think that nothing was as good as "The Man in the Dead Machine." I like the title poem of *The Town of Hill* better than anything else out of that patch. I published these poems because I thought that they were good . . . (I've often been wrong; I've published many poems in magazines that I later left out of books; in the old *New Yorker* anthology, half my poems weren't good enough to put into a book.) Also I published to cheer myself up in a bad time, an ignoble reason but maybe effective. *The Town of Hill* is not my best work, but when Godine bought it I was released into the long line of "Kicking the Leaves." If I had not rid the house of those floundering poems, I'm not sure I could have written the new ones.

RECTOR: *The One Day* works with the kind of 'multiple pro-tagonist' voice we find in "The Waste Land." Why did you make this choice, rather than staying in the fairly mono-lyrical voice which had characterized much of your work?

HALL: Picasso said that every human being is a colony. An old friend of mine said that she was not a person but ran a boarding-house. One of the many problems with the "mono-lyrical" is that it pretends that each of us is singular.

RECTOR: Your work is your church. Have you always been Christian? How does being a Christian enter your work? Isn't the absence of a god (or gods) or an agnosticism an important part of much contemporary poetry? How do you see your work amidst that? If it is something you shy from speaking of, why do you shy from it? Better left unsaid, bad manners, or just refusing to talk about politics and religion at the dinner table?

HALL: I was brought up a Christian, suburban Protestant variety. When I was twelve I converted myself to atheism. During the years I spent in the English village of Thaxted, I used to go to church every Sunday, telling myself that I went because the carving and architecture were so beautiful, because I loved the Vicar (high church and a Communist), because the ceremony was beautiful ... Now I think I was kidding myself, in saying that my feelings were aesthetic. Yes, I am shy of speaking about it. The figure of Jesus is incredibly important, the astonishing figure from the Gospels. I used to think that people who went to church were either swallowing everything or pretending to, hypocritically. Now I know that intelligent practicing Christians often feel total spiritual drought and disbelief; still, even in such moments, ancient ritual and story can be entered, practiced, listened to, considered ...

RECTOR: Not too long ago you did a review of small, literary presses for *Iowa Review*. John Hollander has said that when he was first publishing you could count on a few of the elders to let you know what kind of noises your work was making. Very few older writers now review the work of younger writers, or emerging presses, except to write blurbs for them. Why is this? What is your 'policy' about writing blurbs, and why?

HALL: Thirty years ago I was asked to write blurbs for a few books. I was flattered to be asked, and wrote the blurbs. When the books came out I looked like an ass. Then I looked at other people's blurbs; *they* looked like asses. There are some honorable exceptions but almost every blurb is foolish. The formula for a blurb is an adjective, an adverb, and a verb which usually combine opposites. X is both free-swinging and utterly orderly; Y is classic and romantic; Z is high and at the same time, amazingly, low. Many book reviewers review blurbs rather than the poetry. Blurbs are the Good Housekeeping Seal of Approval. I think it's far worse in poetry than it is in fiction or anything else. Although doubtless many poets write blurbs out of generosity, it doesn't look that way; it gives vent to the widespread notion that poets live by taking in each other's laundry. It hurts poetry. It's done because publishers are too lazy to name what they're printing. Almost always, it would be better to print a poem or an excerpt from a poem . . . but, oh, these terrible blurbs. I refuse to do it.

Although I've refused 2,457 times, although I've written essays against the practice, I still receive two hundred and fifty or three hundred requests a year to write blurbs. How could I add three hundred books and three hundred mini-essays to my life every year? This is *not* my reason for refusing to do them but it would be reason enough. When publishers quote from reviews, excerpts from journalistic occasions, nobody can stop them. Blurbs are *pseudo*-reviews, and they appear to be used in lieu of dinner invitations, thank-you letters, and gold stars. They're nacreous.

Reviewing is in terrible shape. There's more poetry than

ever — more readings, more books, more *sales* of books — and less reviewing. And worse reviewing. Literary journalists like Malcolm Cowley, Louise Bogan, and Edmund Wilson made their living, in large part, by writing book reviews. Their descendants have tenure instead and teach Linebreaks 101. *The New Yorker* by appointing Helen Vendler resigned from reviewing poetry. *Atlantic* and *Harper's* and the old *Saturday Review* reviewed poetry; no more. *The New York Review of Books* isn't interested in poetry and it is stupid when it pretends to. *The New York Times* is at its worst on poetry, especially under the current editor. What's left? *The New Republic* and *The Nation* are honorable; there are the quarterlies, each of them read by few people. *APR* reviews little. We suffer from a lack of intelligent *talk* about poetry. I don't know why. Maybe it's the same cultural separatism that splits creative writing and literature in the university, an epidemic of ignorance, willful know-nothingism. Many young poets if they criticize poetry at all adhere to the philosophy of the booster club, Boost Don't Knock. When Vendler is the leading critic of contemporary poetry we're in a bad way. She can write a sentence but she has *no taste*. She's a bobbysoxer for poets she croons over: some good, some bad, she can't tell the difference. I can't imagine why she chose this line of work.

RECTOR: You went to Harvard with Ashbery, Bly, O'Hara, Koch, Davison, Rich, and others. You said you dated Adrienne Rich. More to say on The Poet's Theatre started there?

HALL: Harvard 1947 to '51 was a lively place. There was a wonderful independent theater group, down at the Brattle. We started the Poet's Theater out of the coincidence of theatrical and poetic activity, and the momentary ascendency of poor old Christopher Fry; of course Eliot worked at poetic drama. Now the Poet's Theater never produced anything memorable but it was another center where energy gathered.

At the *Advocate* we sat around and argued all night. Koch, Ashbery, Bly. Of course O'Hara was around, and Rich. Bly became my best friend. He and I doubledated, with Rich my date. I think Adrienne and I went out twice. At least once I was *awful*: I got pissed and argued with Bly, showing off. Adrienne was *polite*. Much later, when I was married and at Oxford and she was living there as a Guggenheim Fellow, we got to be friends, and we were close for quite a while. I feel gratitude to her, and affection . . . Bly remains my best friend. O'Hara and I were friends for a while, then we quarreled over something or other . . . He was wonderfully funny and alert and lively, a nifty spirit. Ashbery was intelligent and quiet and smart and talented. It was a good time. We competed, you might say.

RECTOR: You've championed the work of poets as different as Robert Creeley and Geoffrey Hill. What accounts for the catholicity of your taste?

HALL: Sometimes I fear that my catholicity is another name for mindlessness . . . but I don't *really* think so. I like to say things like, "If you can't admire both Hill and Creeley, you can't read poetry." (That isn't true either.) Hell, Creeley resembles nobody so much as Henry James. Take a late Henry James sentence and break it into two or three word lines and see what you get. Hill makes the tensest language in the universe, with more sparks flying between adjacent words than any other poet since Andrew Marvell. Both are geniuses. Of course they can't read each other. I'm delighted to say that Helen Vendler can't read either of them.

RECTOR: Who do you think of now as the most interesting men or women of letters? Do you think the person of letters is a kind of vanishing beast?

HALL: People have been talking about the disappearance of the Man of Letters ever since Uncle Matthew died. There has been an All Points Bulletin out, for more than a century. People resurrect the phrase when they want to praise somebody who writes more than one thing: Edmund Wilson, Lionel Trilling. But we have candidates even now: Sven Birkerts in his mid-thirties writes essays about reading, writes criticism about fiction in a hundred languages, writes essays about poetry . . . Lately, many younger poets in America, male and female, spread out doing writing besides poetry — fiction, essays, criticism. *Good!* You learn about your primary art by practicing or investigating other arts — especially others that use language. Now "man of letters" is a fine phrase but it would be a pompous label to put on yourself. Instead, you can call yourself a literary journalist. (Maybe when you're eighty you can call yourself a man or woman of letters.) Let writers come out from under the Rock of the University of America! Let them stick their noses under the rock of the buggy world! Let them make a living by writing.

RECTOR: How do you avoid the whining and the bitterness?

HALL: Well, to start with, I whine bitterly a whole lot . . . They *are* a waste, and they hurt — reason enough to avoid them. You feel bitter about trivial things: *They* have left you out of the Final Anthology — the last bus to the Immortality Graveyard.

Or: Everybody *else* gets this prize.

But . . . there are things I try to remember, which help: ALL prizes are rubber medals. All grapes are sour as soon as you taste them. I haven't won the Pulitzer; if I ever win it, within five minutes I will recollect all the dopes, idiots, time-servers, and class-presidents of poetry who have won the Pulitzer; I will know that getting the Pulitzer means that I'm not damned good. Needless to say, I still want to undergo this disillusion!

Also, it matters to remember: *You're never going to know whether you're good.* Nothing in the inside world stays secure. Nothing in the outside world — like three Nobels for literature in a row, retiring the trophy; like the sale of one million copies of your collected poems in two weeks; like effigies of your person selling in K-Marts from coast to coast — will convince you that you're any damned good. So: give up the notion; what's left? What's left is work.

Of course you still feel annoyance and anger when you're abused. When somebody says something nasty, you can't get the tune out of your head. Words burn themselves into your brain the way an electric needle burns a slogan onto pine; you etch-a-sketch the unforgiveable words onto your skull. It would be good not to read reviews but it's impossible, because if a critic gets nasty there's someone out there who'll xerox the worst parts and mail them to you. The emperor was right to execute the messenger.

But . . . I know so many aging poets, who ream their brains out with rage over mistreatment, neglect, slights both imagined and true. A terrible thing to watch! Because I've seen it so much, I extend energy fending rage off — whining and bitterness — within myself, explaining to myself, over and over again, how the reputation stockmarket rises and falls as irrationally as Wall Street does; remembering literary history and all the *famous* poets no one has heard of; reminding myself: *Get back to work.*

COMMENTARY II

THE NOBLE MAN IN THE SICK PLACE

֍ **Robert McDowell** ֍

There is more than a little truth to the notion that one writes poetry to diagnose and cure a sickness. But only the very best poets of any historical period, in finding the key to their personal maladies, pick their way back to the larger world and contribute to its own perpetual healing.

That existence is cyclical is true, after all. The world goes on endlessly living and dying and we miniscule, poignant, and ridiculous human specks have no choice but to follow suit. I suppose that every generation has been tempted by the sentimental notion that a cure for the down side of the cycle is just around the corner. In the twenties, post-war euphoria and unbridled money speculation reflected a general American feeling that good times would last forever; after the defeat of the Axis powers in the second world war, a more muscularly complacent sense of the good times gripped this country and did not weaken for a decade or more; in the sixties the *bad* times — Viet Nam, Civil Rights, the Cold War — were so bad that with characteristic American initiative many citizens packaged, advertized, bought and sold them, making them seem almost good. It was a time to be *committed*, good to be *high*, good to be *righteously apart*. By the late seventies the common cure for the cycle's down side was to feel good about yourself. Self-help became an industry, the full flowering of America's long adolescent passage.

Every culture, every country, every man and woman and artist must pass this way. But successfully crossing the bridge between adolescence and maturity requires that cultures and coun-
tries, individuals and artists put away childish things. The life
cycle, if not celebrated, is respected for its darkness as well as
its light. If pain and loss are always frightening, they are also
essential in that they create a context for joy. And like the many
complex stages of dying—the dying that takes a lifetime to
accomplish—they are *natural*.

Having accepted this condition, perhaps the mature poet
probes his own sickness to discover what he loves most outside
himself. Whether or not he succeeds is the work of a lifetime,
and in many cases the final judgement is rendered posthumously.
The down side of the life cycle will not be altered by the luck
and genius of his pen. But if his work succeeds in speaking to
and for individual conditions within the grand condition of
his generation, if it succeeds in casting into high relief those
insignificant dramas, the work will have contributed to our long
historical labors toward wisdom.

By such turns is the world improved. It is impossible to say
that most poets of our time are building such a contribution.
I might add historical weight to this statement with the obvious
fact that most poets of previous times have been long and
justifiably forgotten. In Posterity's sideshow most poets will
vanish, and with them will go the vast majority of their critical
champions and detractors.

But if the poet whose work survives could catch a glimpse
of the entire journey, he might very well be staggered by the
vision of a perilous hall of mirrors. In this reflective, distorted
corridor he might see that the mature poet is many fractured
selves speaking with one cohesive voice. He might see that he

must be part of his culture's time and condition and simultaneously outside them.

If it is impossible to predict with blessed finality who among our living poets will successfully navigate that corridor, it is easy for me to play a hunch and put forth the work of a poet whose ten published volumes so clearly document the poet's difficult journey from adolescence to maturity.

When Donald Hall published *Exiles and Marriages* in 1955, he enjoyed what most young poets dream of, the launch of one's career by a major press (Viking). A graduate of Harvard and Oxford, Hall at a very early age had already achieved an enviable high visibility and authority. In the next three years the publication of his second book, *The Dark Houses*, and the powerful *New Poets of England and America*, which he edited with Robert Pack and Louis Simpson, solidified his leading position in American letters and fulfilled the promise of his auspicious debut. At the same time, Hall became a major source of information concerning what was going on in the contemporary poetry of England, and he soon began an esteemed academic career at the University of Michigan. In every respect he seemed to have plucked the prizes along the fast track of a traditional career in letters. Very early on he found himself an honored man.

But it is a fact of American life that the successful and busy are simultaneously admired and hated. Where at first Hall's poetry was celebrated for its craft, wit, and honesty, the next wave of attention brought up charges that the work was derivative, flat, or self-consciously weighty. The honored man of letters was much maligned.

This is only one of the many trials by fire that the mature poet and noble person must go through. Honor, as we know, is often bestowed arbitrarily by others, but nobility is the consequence of a moral, generous life and its work carried on without compromise — or at least lasting compromise. It is safe to say that the poet who actively seeks nobility rarely finds it. All the poet can do is seek answers to the dilemmas of his time and propose humane alternatives to brutish, simplistic solutions. Nobility cannot be granted by committee.

At the same time, it is the honor of awards that promotes academic careers, secures readings and residencies, insures a poem's appearance in the "definitive" anthologies of the day. Small wonder, then, that these honors often enjoy more value in our society than nobility.

This situation seems to have dogged Donald Hall's middle poetry, and though some of the specific criticism leveled against that work was valid, the impulse behind the attacks was entirely wrongheaded. Only with the publication of the last three volumes (beginning with *Kicking the Leaves* in 1978) have critics begun to examine the coherent developments, from first book to last, of this important poet's work, work that in his own words aimed at "the bone that showed in each deliberate word."

This line appears in "An Elegy for Wesley Wells," which was printed in Hall's first book. This collection, in the best and worst sense, is a young man's ardent effort. The first of seven sections includes the fine "Conduct and Work," the equally superb "The Columns of the Parthenon" (though its impact is diminished by its unforunate, short last three lines), "A Child's Garden," which unites a grandfather's death with the death of childhood and hauntingly foreshadows the later work, and the supple brief ballad "Iuvenes Dum Sumus," in which we observe the poignant progression of young love to old age: "They walk in the weather of pain."

In these opening poems, especially, the young poet Donald

Hall discovered his two general and timeless subjects and began to make flesh of his own articulation about them. He explored the nature of love, the essential condition that breaks and builds us, and he confronted the conflict of generations, though *conflict* suggests more rebellion than I mean and none of the reverence that is all important in this poet's work. When he treated the latter subject, his aim was to raise a bridge connecting himself to the generations ahead of him and those behind. At their best, the poems seem to contain both subjects, as if they were sewn together.

Farther on in the book, in "September Ode" for example, the poet is concerned with love as a fleeting condition, but one which ends in the jealousy of a dying old age. The focus is on rooms "cluttered with the truth of years, / Possessions of the unreturn-ing blood." In the fairy tale "The Sleeping Giant" the narrator is a child of four and a New England hill is personified. Early on the landscape of home is alive, magical, a character as animated as the people who walk it. Here we are introduced to the land as conduit between one generation and the next. In an earlier poem, "New England November," the outcast made separate by the condition of age (childhood) becomes the outcast made separate by the condition of travel. Though in England, the adult exile-narrator remembers with reverence the house of the father, the house of the grandfather. In "My Son, My Executioner" a father and mother "Observe enduring life in you / And start to die together." One generation must move on, in service to the life cycle, making room for the next. All that exists for the diligent traveler on this path is the wish "May I earn / An honest eye." Finally, "Wedding Speeches," a dialogue between a bride and groom, is a clear precurser to the "Pastoral" section of *The One Day*, which will see publication more than three decades later.

If in the early poems Hall begins to wrestle with the subjects that will mark his maturity he is also grappling with healthy, unfocused ambition. So much is included in the exhuberant *Exiles and Marriages* that the reader's eye and ear can be distracted by the variety of subject and style. Poems involving Hall's strongest subject are interspersed with lighter poems of wit and satire like "The Lone Ranger" and "Six Poets in Search of a Lawyer." Formal stanzas and syllabics at times overwhelm individual poems. This versatility — what might be admiringly discussed as *range* in the work of an older poet — in a younger poet is often criticized as confusion, and confusion certainly contributes to the situation. And if the poet's progress is good, he feels most keenly the lash of loose ends and moves to anchor them to his own design.

In Hall's case this confrontation would eventually lead to years of painstaking revision and experiment, but in his second book it led to an arbitrary division of subject and inclination. "Houses on Residential Streets" and "Men, Alone," the two sections of *The Dark Houses* (1958) read more like separate books than parts of a sustained collection.

In the first section the narrator is the grown-up suburban kid finding fault with his home town and yearning for the summer farm "where nothing and no one ever came to harm." Perhaps most powerful among the solid poems in this section is "Christmas Eve in Whitneyville," a bitter elegy for the poet's father, dead at fifty-two, and for the town itself. Recalling the loveliness of the place and resigned to the changes wrought by the wars, the narrator concludes that "now Whitneyville is like the other places." Not satisfied with this rather common lament, the poet pushes harder for a more difficult truth and remembers that even before the wars Whitneyville was a town "settled with the men / who worked at mass-producing firearms." Our doom is in our innocent, harmless beginnings and in our labor as we make the monster we cannot see until it is too late. In "Religious Articles" a young man in the local church hears the dead voices of his tribe beside him in the pew as they tell him that "We who do not exist make noises / only in you." The poet must preserve the flawed history of an important place and its people by speaking for the silenced ones and listening well, always listening.

Even when the poet is disappointed, he must see the root of disappointment in himself, not in his subjects, and tell the truth. In "The Clock-Keeper," the poet accompanies his grand-father on a visit to Jim Hout in 1938. Hout is a veteran of the Spanish-American war and a champion wrestler whose house contains one hundred forty-nine clocks. The boy, having imagined a hero, is dismayed to meet "an old, / red-faced, fat, womanish creature" in slippers who praises Teddy Roosevelt but harangues Franklin D. The grandfather is shaken, too, by this timekeeper damaged by war and punished by time. Imprisoned and doomed by the thing he keeps, Hout most resembles the inhabitants of the big clock he got at the World's Fair: "small people / marched out of it resolutely, did / their duty, and retired to some cell."

These poems are deeply personal and yet succeed in speaking clearly to anyone who has been involved in a community. The poems in the "Men Alone" section, however, are most self-conscious in intent and distant in tone. It is as if the poet has momentarily yielded to the temptation to speak *wisely* about his fellows. At times the meter and rhyme are weighty, the rhetoric forced, unnatural.

In his introduction to *Contemporary American Poetry* (1962),

Hall named Robert Lowell and Richard Wilbur as the two poets who "form the real beginning of post-war American poetry because they are the culmination of past poetries." Lowell's *Lord Weary's Castle* was "a monument of the line of tough rhetoricians;" Wilbur's *The Beautiful Changes* "was the peak of skillful elegance." In the second section of *The Dark Houses* Hall seems to be making his most conscious effort to ram the two together. But what was not so clear to Hall in 1962 (or to anyone) was that Lowell's serious character flaws frequently undermined the subjects of his poems while Wilbur's subjects were deliberately *small*. No synthesis of the two was coherently possible or necessary, though the serious poet of the fifties had to confront the issue.

By the time *A Roof of Tiger Lilies* appeared in 1964, Hall at mid-life had come to the end of his first substantial writing period. This book does contain a few poems that treat Hall's preoccupation with generations. "The Days" and "In the Kitchen of the Old House" are the best examples. The latter poem contains these beautiful lines in which a man comes upon the house where he was born and experiences love in recollection: "as if the city and the house / were closed inside a globe which I shook / to make it snow." "The Stump," a typically (for Hall) moving country elegy is also noteworthy in this vein. Also present in this volume are lighter poems of satire, Hall's first experiments with the Deep Image, and political poems.

A poem from the first category such as "Christ Church Meadows, Oxford" displays Hall's good humor at its best. In it a gauche American tourist faints and is cast into the waters by order of the Yank she's mistaken for an Englishman of importance. Poems like "The Husbands" and "The Wives," however, are standard *list* poems that were fashionably popular in the sixties and seventies.

If these last poems displayed some of the formulaic flaws of the Deep Image, Hall's serious flirtation with this method produced some of his better poems to date. "The Tree and the Cloud," "The Sun," "The Moon," "The Child," "The Sea," and "The Kill" are notable for their imagery and ominous myth-making. What allows Hall to transcend the usual limits of the Deep Image poem (superficial emotion, formulaic constructions) is his innate storytelling gift, which makes it difficult for him to settle only for surfaces in the landscapes of these poems.

Finally, as did many poets of the sixties, Hall attempted to present a more visible political awareness in poems like "An Airstrip in Essex, 1960" and "The Assassin." In connection with this endeavor a worldly malevolence asserted itself more strongly here than in any collection to date (see "The Kill"), and counterbalancing it was a kind of popular primitivism of the period, a yearning for some earlier time and place before the complex world confounded us. In being seduced by this romantic primitivism, which we can now see as the obvious precursor to the nostalgia craze that gripped us in the eighties, Hall was not alone. But as a poem like "Eating the Pig" demonstrated more than a decade later, he was one of the few who did not settle down, content to utter the same formulaic expression over and over.

Indeed, the poet of *A Roof of Tiger Lilies* seems restless, playing the field of subjects and forms. In *The Alligator Bride: Poems New & Selected* (1969), the experimental impulse turns back on past poems and settles on free verse in new ones. In the first two sections, which reprint poems from the first three books, the poet calls on the craft and maturity he has won to get it right. By cutting the second stanza of "Wedding Party," for example, he removes the narrator and widens the poem's focus. The last stanza of "My Son, My Executioner" has also been cut to remove stilted rhetoric. The final preachy couplet of "Je Suis une Table" also disappears. Even the small change in "Christmas Eve in Whitneyville" is significant: "Across America" becomes "All over Whitneyville." The revision is more accurate and resists the young man's tendency to generalize and lecture. Almost all of Hall's revisions improve the early work, though when the long poem "Exile" is chopped down to three couplets something valuable is lost. And it is reassuring to see that the poet knew enough to leave a poem like "The Sleeping Giant" alone.

The twenty-five new poems in "The Alligator Bride" section say goodbye to the rhyme and traditional meters of the early poems but not to their subjects. The poem "Woolworth's" is preoccupied with generations—"Three hundred years ago I was hedging / and ditching in Devon." "The Table" is a lovely reminiscence of the poet's grandfather and his legendary workhorse, Old Riley. "Pictures of Philippa" focuses on the poet's daughter and his role as father. "Apples" and "Mount Kearsarge" are set in the vicinity of the ancestral farm. To a great extent, these poems work because a personal, localized sense of history—and by extension the history of our country—is alive in them.

The weaker poems in this new section, like "The Alligator Bride," suffer under the weight of surrealism and the Deep Image. The language sounds constricted and self-conscious, the insights no deeper than those generated only by casual observation. As a group these poems suggest that the poet is reaching for a new breakthrough of subject and style consistent with the experiments that characterized much of the American poetry written in the sixties.

As he observes others keeping the past alive, he sees more clearly how to celebrate and salvage his own roots.

This is the lesson that a community, even a community of departed ancestors, can teach an individual. In "Maple Syrup" the narrator and his wife, in exploring the ancestral farmhouse they've returned to, discover an old jar of maple syrup prepared by a grandfather years ago. The narrator sees it as the sweetness representing what is best in life. As a gift from a cherished relation, it is made all the sweeter because it is unexpected. It is the gift of the old to the young. Or as the poet puts it elsewhere, in "Stone Walls": "riding home from the hayfields, he handed me the past."

These and other poems here like "Ox Cart Man," "Names of Horses," "The Black Faced Sheep," and "Traffic" are the unself-conscious work of a poet who knows his subject and believes in it. Celebratory, elegiac, they are remarkably rich in sentiment and refreshingly devoid of the borrowed emotion that is sentimentality.

This self-assurance translates smoothly to *The Happy Man* (1986), which both picks up and extends the subjects of *Kicking the Leaves* and foreshadows the book-length *The One Day*.

Arranged in four sections, *The Happy Man* begins with a group of poems under the heading "Barnyards." So we find ourselves back in the loving muck and richness of the preceding volume. Of the best poems here, "Great Day in the Cow's House" is a companion piece to "Names of Horses," but it has more depth:

> They are long dead; they survive, in the great day
> that cancels the successiveness of creatures.

In "Whip-poor-will" the narrator encounters a ghost bird that seems to call his grandfather's name. "Twelve Seasons," "The Henyard Round," "The Rocker," and "New Animals" present the familiar ancestral land and the rock-hard characters that held and worked it. "New Animals" also serves to demonstrate the poet's method of revision, for its first half is lifted and recast from the prose piece "Flies" in *Kicking the Leaves*.

The book's second section, "Shrubs Burnt Away," consists of one long passage from a book-length poem and represents Hall's most ambitious use of dramatic monologue. Two characters, a man and a woman, tell in alternate passages the stories of their lives.

The man in middle age remembers a father who was "bullied, found wanting," who drove home "from his work at the lumberyard weeping." Identifying with this father's frustration, with increasing bitterness the man tells of leaving his family, veering off into alcohol and rented rooms, bottoming out in the Hollywood-La Brea Motel:

> . . . Studying a bikini'd
> photograph on a match box, I dial BONNIE FASHION
> MODEL AVAILABLE at four in the morning
> from my vinyl room, and the answering service tells me
> that Bonnie is out to lunch . . .

Later he tells us "The world is a bed," our lives dull tracks on which "we perform procedures of comfort."

The woman, a sculptor, recalls a nearly fatal childhood illness, a frustrated mother, one "summer on the farm, / painting water-colors all morning, all afternoon hoeing / the garden with my grandmother who told stories," marriages, divorces, and children.

Both speakers share a desperate need to make sense of the assault that is collective experience, and in struggle to do so they "daydream the house of dying: The colony takes comfort / in building this house which does not exist, because / it does not exist." Significant in their struggle is the sheer balance in the poet's conception of the parts they play. Each is explicit and comprehensive in confession. This balance and concision represent the poet's most successful attempt to speak for a larger community, by faithfully presenting the life conditions of its inhabitants. After mastering the subject of the home this step outward, into the community, is a breakthrough.

The Happy Man's third section, "Men Driving Cars," continues this exploration of the larger world and is as much a success as the section it echoes from an earlier book ("Men Alone" in *The Dark Houses*) was a failure. The poems here extend the male walk through the wilderness introduced by the man in the book's preceding section. In "Mr. Wakeville on Interstate 90" a man loses his family, becomes a stranger in the community, and concludes that "There will be no room inside me for other places." In "My Friend Felix" the narrator on a long drive fondly remembers a dead friend but must come back to the lonely hush of the closed car. The perspective on isolation and mortality is further heightened in "Old Timer's Day at Fenway" as we witness the spectacle of Ted Williams ("the ruin / of even the bravest / body") laboring to catch a fly ball. Appropriately, the narrator thinks of Odysseus glimpsing the shadow of Achilles in the Underworld. In such comparison lies salvation for those who fear that we are *always* alone.

The book's concluding section, "Sisters," circles back to the family and includes three exceptional poems, "A Sister on the Tracks," the seven part "A Sister By the Pond," and "The Day I Was Older." The business of these poems is the "soul's ascension connecting dead to unborn."

> . . . Here love builds
> its mortal house, where today's wind carries
> a double scent of heaven and cut hay.

(from A Sister on the Tracks)

This stay against loneliness, against meaninglessness, is really our only option. In "The Day I Was Older" the poet relies on traditional symbols (the clock, the news, the pond, the day, the cup) to promote this view. In the poem the grandfather, father, and children all come back, merging with the narrator who himself is part and parcel, only a temporary conduit in the one timeless body. This is the redemptive condition that comes of the earlier bitter confession.

The Happy Man both consolidates the poet's mastery of the subjects of home and family and introduces a powerful effort to link the conditions found in these subjects to a larger landscape.

In *The One Day* (1988), a three part book-length sequence, the complicated sexual, psychological, and political implications of characters populating that landscape compel the reader to reconsider not only his own inner life but the teeming world around him. It is a world in which corruption and failure dominate.

Earlier I discussed the book's first section, "Shrubs Burnt Away" (changed from "Shrubs Burned Away" in *The Happy Man*) in the context of its perfect balance. This balanced double portrayal might be said to indict the sexual roles we learn to play. If we admit a political element to sexuality the book's second section, "Four Classic Texts," shifts this element to center stage. Here is the beginning of the first monologue:

> I will strike down wooden houses; I will burn aluminum
> clapboard skin; I will strike down garages

> where crimson Toyotas sleep side by side; I will explode
> palaces of gold, silver, and alabaster: — the summer
> great house and its folly together.

Such aggressive, elegant cataloguing has not appeared in American poetry since Whitman. After returning to his own beginnings and coming to terms with them, the poet confronts the greed and willfulness of the greater modern world.

In "Pastoral," the second of these *Texts*, criticism focuses on a contemporary upwardly mobile couple, Marc and Phyllis, whose alternating monologues are as funny as they are disturbing. Here are Marc's opening lines:

> Shepherd and shepherdess, I with my pipe and song,
> you leaning on your crook, in the kitchen's
> hot galley among slaveboys and electric knives....

These are people with status ("I live in an unfenced compound among swineherds / and milkmaids identical in age, income, and education. / I am unacquainted with anyone . . . whom I fear and despise."); they punctually go through the motions ("we pull off our clothes like opening junk mail."); and in a moment of revelation they face what they've lost ("We forget / every skill we acquired over ten thousand years of labor. / I practice smiling; I forget how to milk a goat.") If the poet's tone makes us smile, we may also feel the urge to weep for these people we know all too well.

"History," the third *Text*, provides depth and background for the opening prophecy and examination of one couple. Senex, a rather sour character, indicts not only the modern world but the ages. Self-interest has always been our primary motivation, deception our favorite tool: "In the execution of governance the expedients / of postponement and triage: — These are the rules of rule."

If we come out of this section feeling the burden of stacked choices heavy on our shoulders, the narrator in "Eclogue" quickly relieves the weight.

> Help me proclaim the child. Not everyone prays for fire
> or adores the styrofoam cup and its trash compactor....

> ...If we praise trees let us praise
> the acorns of generation. While the Sibyl sings
> the music of what happens, while Senex brags and grumbles
> of millenia and legions, the jig of centuries

> slows down, entropy's tune; and I sing before midnight,
> before solstice, when the great year will regenerate....

But before we can "worship creation in faithful skin," the narrator is adamant about our need to overcome "the vector of greed."

In the poem's third and closing section, we return to the monologues of the man and woman of part one. Both are older, and the spirit of resignation and praise fill their speeches. The woman, now a famous sculptor, receives the king and queen of Norway at her studio and prepares to accept a Presidential medal. Early on she sums up the philosophy she's come to: "I marry the creation that stays / in place to be worked at, day after day." The man settles into a New Hampshire farm, reviews his country's and his own past, predicts the coming "days of mourning, long walks growing slow and painful," admits to his contemplation current scenes with his mate, and comes to a simple but profound resolution that not only rights his life's course but can also apply to Donald Hall's long poetic journey: "Two chimneys require: / work, love, build a house, and die. But build a house."

A READING OF DONALD HALL'S
"KICKING THE LEAVES"

Gregory Orr

When William Carlos Williams, in "A Sort of Song," calls on metaphor to "reconcile / the people and the stones," he clearly means by stones the world we inhabit, the world we move through. In that same lyric, Williams proposes a vegetative metaphor for the self, for his self: "Saxifrage is my flower that splits / the rocks." The vitality, almost stubborn muscularity of the metaphor is unmistakable and characteristic. Donald Hall's ambition in his major poem, "Kicking the Leaves," is also expressed through a metaphor from the vegetative world, but Hall's poem aims to reconcile us not to life (Williams' goal) but to death: lives are leaves.

*

"Kicking the Leaves" is a poem of family — four generations of Hall's personal family inhabit its seven sections. But it also belongs to the family of poems. At the source of the poem's unspoken genealogy, its genealogy of imagination, is Homer's famous metaphor from *The Iliad*, where Glaucos, challenged to identify himself by Diomedes, responds:

> "Magnanimous Diomedes, why do you ask who I am? The frail generations of men have scarcely more lineage than leaves. Wind blows them to earth in the fall, but spring brings the blossoms again. So one generation succeeds another."

Reprinted from *The Iowa Review*, Vol. 18, No. 1, by permission of the author. Copyright © 1988 Gregory Orr.

A second sponsor of the leaf metaphor is Hopkins' "Spring and Fall," whose "Leaves like the things of man" is the central imaginative premise for a poem of great elegaic beauty enacted as a child's dawning awareness of the mortality she shares with the world of created beings. But Hopkins' poem, unlike the passage from Homer, is also about human connectedness and awareness of others—for me, the pivotal line in the poem is "And yet you will weep and know why," where the young girl's emotional simplicity breaks through the speaker's self-satisfied philosophizing and demands a more authentic response, one that acknowledges and incorporates the deepest sources of her grief. Hall's poem shares with Hopkins' this awareness of other selves.

*

Leaves. Their very multiplicity, their "droveness," seems to resist transformation into a symbol for the human condition. As if we were accustomed to the lyric symbol which thrives on the precise outline of a single, centered thing—a nightingale, say. It is their resistance, their multiplicity that is a form of the "Kicking the Leaves" generosity. Though the poem's sections tell the story of the generations of Hall's family and of his own life in time from boyhood to age, there is in the image of the multiplicity of leaves a clear sense that Hall is saying: I am only one leaf among all the leaves of human stories. We are half a step from Whitman's central invitation: "What I assume you shall assume, / For every atom belonging to me as good belongs to you."

Hall's generosity, his overcoming of the egocentrism that overwhelms so many lyric enterprises, is not his only accomplishment. As deep as that is his ability to hold the poem together so that it doesn't disperse into drifts and scuds. He does this by staying close to human story—to located anecdote. The poem is anchored in story and anecdote, yet opens up again and again toward mystery, toward the ultimate human mysteries of time and death.

*

It's not exactly news that the central impulse in Donald Hall's work is elegiac — that he is obsessed with elegy as others are said to be obsessed with sex or death. But is is worth noting that "Kicking the Leaves" is the triumphant culmination of this obsession. All his earlier, scattered elegiac occasions are, like raked leaves, gathered in one place: the beloved maternal grandparents and their farm, the father's early death that terrifies the son as predictive of his own, the ambivalent sense of his children's vitality and futurity, and there at the center the self longing to elegize its own perishing and be lifted up into elegy as certain saints were taken up bodily into heaven at the point of death.

*

The poem opens with the long, accumulating, Whitmanic lines that will characterize it as a whole. The first sentence is seven lines long; the second sentence comprises the remaining ten lines of the section.

The initial verb, "kicking," is repeated four times in section one, becoming at the outset the incantatory gesture that initiates the poem's discoveries. The first occasion of kicking the leaves locates the speaker in a moment and place (October, Ann Arbor). The second "kick" leads to an awareness of particular leaves (maple, poplar, elm) and a tentative metaphorical listing. With the third repetition, the poem enacts its central process—the rising up of lost or buried memories and experiences by way of an unconsciously repeated gesture — the emergence of the "involuntary memory" Proust asserted as being central to urgent art. The sound of kicking the leaves triggers associated memories that transport us into three places in Hall's past: walking to school as a boy in Connecticut, roadside New Hampshire, and finally Massachusetts in 1955. We are always located geographically in section one and these four places are and will remain the poem's cardinal points.

We could say the language unfolds under the momentum of the sound and gesture of the repeated "kick," until each sentence arrives at the poem's obsessive center: death. The listing of specific leaves and their metaphors gets no further than three, stops (as does the sentence) at the elm's, whose fatal blight occasions the metaphor. Likewise the second sentence, with its unfolding memories, also ends with the awareness of the father's impending death.

*

How the poem accumulates and accretes by its dependent clauses — "from the game, in Ann Arbor, / on a day the color of soot, rain in the air. . . . " If this was sculpture, Hall's style would be that of a modeler, not a carver; rather than stripping away toward a lyric center, he slaps on phrase after phrase like lumps of clay, building his shape gradually. Each phrase adding, modifying, locating — always locating and making local. How powerfully that strategy is a work in the opening of section two:

> Each fall in New Hampshire, on the farm
> Where my mother grew up, a girl in the country.

Section two is structured around two anecdotes. The general ("Each fall") segueing into the particular ("One November . . ."), even as the grandson replaces his mother and thus preserves the basic family unit at their tasks — achieving an intimacy and harmony based on proximity and shared labor:

Three of us sitting together, silent, in gray November.

And always the clauses and phrases — clustering, accumulating, layering like leaves, modifying — here undercutting, there aggrandizing — always going on and on — a poem built on commas.

In secton two the leaves are a minor, naturalistic part of the farm's dynamic life. They have a function — to insulate the house in winter, preserve its heat. In this section the reader becomes aware of how much of the poem relies on the power of descriptive language.

*

Section three presents another triadic anecdote, again particularized by its prepositional phrases: "One Saturday when I was little, before the war . . . ." The whole anecdote/section is a single sentence, revealing the unity of the poem's stylistic and thematic strategy: to bind together in a single unit of speech the disparate figures and facts — a wholeness out of the bits of bright fact and memory, the scattered remnants of mortality — leaves gathered up into the single pile of the sentence.

The anecdote of this triad (father, son, mother) is of an interactive intimacy, not just the silent parallel labor of section two. The father plays with the son, makes contact with him; the mother "sees" them and responds with both pleasure and concern. Since this is elegy, concern has the final work: ". . . afraid I would fall and be hurt."

*

Section four returns to the opening scene of section one,

echoing the opening phrase: "Kicking the leaves today, as we walk home together." Now the poem's guiding, overarching metaphor begins to assert itself: the connections between the human world and the world of leaves. The stepping stone to this is the football pennants "as many and bright as leaves." From there to the third triadic arrangement of people: father (speaker), daughter, and son. People are like trees: the daughter like a birch; the son, a maple. Again, we have the triad of a basic family unity, but here the speaker, for all his joy and pride in his children (expressed in the flattery of the similes) is about to become the locus of loss. The triad is not that of the child (speaker) and two parents (section three) or the youth (speaker) and his grandparents (section two), where the focus was on the child. Here it is the speaker as parent and his two children and their futurity points away from him as the point of origin. It is an "unstable" triangle, a triad of imminent loss.

Sentence one (nine and a half lines) culminates in the grown son's eagerness to depart the family. Sentence two (the next nine lines, the rest of the section) focuses on the father ("I") as he experiences the vertigo of loss. Standing by a totem pile of leaves, he watches their departure ("their shapes grown small with distance") and recognizes in it his own diminishment and mortality. In an early, grimly elegant and witty poem, "My Son, My Executioner," the "birth" of one generation was seen as representing the death of the other, parental generation and gave a sinister, darkly Freudian undertone to Hall's elegiac impulse. But here, in "Kicking the Leaves" we are outside in the sun and fresh air of autumn, not trapped in the claustrophobic lucubrations of the self alone with its thoughts in a closed house. Here, the intimations of mortality are seen and accepted: "as I go first / into the leaves, taking / the step they will follow. . . ."

At first, "into the leaves" seems a euphemism for "into the ground," "into the grave," but it is one of the poem's burdens and triumphs to make the descent into the leaves as believable an imaginative possibility as it was when first presented to us in section three as the naturalistic possibility of a kid tumbling in leaves with his father. By section six, the leaves will become the entrance to the underworld of the dead. And by section seven, they will have expanded to become not just a pile of leaves, but an entire ocean — an elemental, the elemental entity and emblem for the human condition of mortality as all pervasive and insisted upon as Whitman's grass in his great celebratory elegy, "Song of Myself."

*

The opening line of section five picks up and transforms the last line/gesture of section one; here, instead of the father's death, we have the "birth" of poems, the "rebirth" of poems and creativity.

Sections five and six break the pattern on the long opening sentence — in fact, the first lines of both sections are end-stopped sentences.

For the first time, the poem shifts away from family memory and family event by introducing the theme of poetry: "This year the poems came back, when the leaves fell." One purpose of elegy is to articulate a loss and then locate a consolation for that loss. Although "Kicking the Leaves" has extended its elegiac ambition widely (and will, by poem's end, extend it even further), the end of section four has temporarily focused the imminent loss in the person of the speaker himself — it is he who will "go first / into the leaves." From this loss that is one's own death emerges the consolation that has always created and defined the personal poet: poems.

Only at the very moment that this consolation asserts itself most strongly ("I looked up into the maples / and found them, the vowels of bright desire . . . . ") can the speaker acknowledge the horror of the years without poems. The image for this horror, a ghoulish mynah bird/rooster, is ironically located — up among the trees whose leaves are associated with poems, but the branches are bare and such a sinister black bird seems equally at home in the deathful confinement of chicken wire and cinderblock, is in fact at home everywhere, haunting and taunting the speaker with its "red eye with no lid."

If there was any question that the poet's companion bird was an image of life without poems (which is also, the poem would have it, death-in-life), then this is resolved when the word "lid" is repeated three lines after its first appearance with the bird; only now, in the opening lines of section six, it is the lid of a grave.

The red eye is now lidded, but the lids are of graves and the poem, while returning to the family (this time the paternal lineage) will impinge more fatefully than ever on the speaker. Section six seems to assert in an understated way a theory of generational diminishment (grandfather dies at 77, father at 52) and a geographical diminishment as well (from farm to suburbs). These twin diminishments haunt the poet: Johnson's Pond has "surrendered to houses" and the speaker is now intensely aware of approaching the age at which his father died. Numerological doom presides over this section even as the ecstasy of nostalgic intimacy erupts through the middle:

> Oh, how we flung
> leaves in the air! How they tumbled and fluttered around us
> like slowly cascading water, when we walked together . . . .

*

The final section takes its cue from the ecstatic verbs of section six, not its gloomy numbers. The wisdom of verbs espoused here is reminiscent of that in Galway Kinnell's "Another Night in the Ruins" — if we are to be consumed by the fire, we should embrace it and become the fire. But Kinnell's poem, despite its overt rejection of the phoenix as emblem of the self, still believes in a transformative event at the moment of death — the transcendent ascent of annhilation implicit in his governing image of fire. Hall's poem refuses transformation, stays in the human shape, and asserts a descent. The three verbs in the opening line propound a metaphysics of passionate defeat in which gravity (and death) get two verbs and the human will gets one:

> Now I fall, now I leap and fall . . . .

Or we could understand the phrasing as being a statement ("Now I fall") which the poet corrects even as he says it in order to express that his death is not a fate but a willed act: "now I leap and fall."

And the motive for such a gesture is revealed as intensified life: "to feel . . . , to feel."

Now the leaves are everything. Now the leaves that represent the mortal condition are omnipresent — they are night and ocean — a cosmic, solemn, ecstatic vastness into which the individual self is absorbed. We have entered Whitman's imaginative territory here — the shadow Whitman of rapturous elegies whose "Out of the Cradle Endlessly Rocking" finds the sweetest word, the most "delicious" world of all, to be what the waves whisper: "death, death, death, death . . . ."

As with Whitman's poem, there is a sense of death as a being taken back — Hall experiences the death as an ecstatic regression — "the soft laps of leaves." And in fact, as he swims down to the bottom of the leafpile he discovers his grand-parents' farmhouse. Its enclosed intimacy has become all things: womb, tomb, beloved farmhouse of childhood. In a series of essays called *Seasons At Eagle Pond* (Ticknor and Fields, 1987), Hall writes of the joy of New England winters for those who are "darkness-lovers," those who are "partly tuber, partly bear." (Hall has an early poem called "Self-Portrait, As a Bear" and both ingredients of the farmhouse soup — carrots and onions — mature in the earth.) Here dormancy and hibernation and cozy security fuse with nostalgia, and we see that the poem has adopted a strategy Freud recommends and which Hall frequently quotes: regression in the service of the ego. Roethke did the same thing throughout his "Lost Son" sequence — elevated regression to a spiritual and poetic principle.

Another Whitman poem, section six of "Song of Myself," is worth mentioning in connection with this culminating event of Hall's poem. Significantly, it is the section where Whitman first introduces the image of grass as a vehicle for his obsessive concerns, as that thing in the material world that will stand for so much in his metaphysical and imaginative world. It opens: "A child said, 'What is the grass?' fetching it to me with full hands. . . . " No sooner does Whitman express his inability to answer the mystery of the question with descriptive language, then he begins to "guess" what it is with a series of stunning and free-ranging metaphors: a flag, perfumed handkerchief, child, universal hieroglyph. Free-ranging up to a point; for when he arrives at a certain image ("And now it seems to me the beautiful uncut hair of graves"), he has encountered an obsessive theme. From that point on, Whitman's imagination circles around one of his favorite subjects: a sensual death.

Whitman has entered a spiral of obsession—his imagination is no longer free and centrifugal and, for the next 26 lines, he circlingly descends toward his still point of obsession and the poem's final line: "And to die is different from what any one supposed, and luckier."

Hall, too, in the final section of "Kicking the Leaves," has entered the spiral of obsession; he, too, is drawn down as if in a whirlpool—"swooping in long glides to the bottom."

Leaves are Hall's sea, not grass as in Whitman. There is no implied rebirth here, no hint of reincarnation no matter how diffuse, no "if you want me again look for me under your boot-soles." In Hall, the image of leaves, like Hopkins' Goldengrove that "leafmeal lies," cannot be imagined as leading beyond death. Presumably, Hopkins' Christianity tells him that death is not the end, that the soul rises afterward. Hall has no such faith and for him the final ecstatic celebration of leaves and death is inextricably bound up with the consoling regressive fantasy of the farmhouse at the very bottom of the whirlpool's funnel—a personal and particular focus of intimacy. The image of this whirlpool spiral is important—it indicates that death is not a scattering of the objects and meanings of life, but a centripetal funneling, an ingathering of them.

*

Hall's poem accepts but transforms Homer's great metaphor. The generations of men are as leaves. But one can give assent—can leap as well as fall: the heroic acceptance of destiny. One could even argue that the Homeric consolation of leaving a name in the tribal epic through heroic behavior is also a consolation Hall's poem seeks: " The pleasure, the only long pleasure, of taking a place / in the story of leaves." But it would be important to stress the central feel of Hall's poem: not of Homer's heroic warriors, but of family intimacy and connection; a constant linking across generations, as families can do, as leaves and warriors cannot.

WORKING WELL, WORKING WRONG:
SOME DISTINCTIONS
IN DONALD HALL'S *THE ONE DAY*

❧ Joyce Peseroff ☙

Driving one afternoon to my office in Concord, Massachusetts, I noticed that the old house and barn with the "For Sale" sign in front had been knocked into a pile of timber flecked with red paint. Two days later the timber was gone, replaced by a hole. Over the next weeks foundation was laid, frames erected, walls set up, roof raised. Quickly, on the site of that modest farmstead, rose an edifice built for giants, to go by proportions: the roofbeam twice the height of its neighbors, and the chimney twice as wide. From the triple garage to the double-portaled front door, everything about the house seemed excessive and outsized.

I reasoned that it cost a little more to frame a big house than a small one, and a bit more to finish ten large rooms than six, and that installing a $700 dishwasher rather than the $400 model might raise the property's asking price another $1000. . . . Why build anything humbler, since anything less would deliver less than maximum profit to the builder?

> Or: borrow to buy fifty acres of pasture from the widower:
> Survey, cut a road, sub-divide; bulldoze the unpainted
> barn, selling eighteenth century beams with bark
> still on them . . . .

> . . . Build huge
> centrally heated colonial ranches — brick, stone and wood
> confounded together — on old pasture slopes that were white
> with clover . . . .

So Donald Hall, in his new book-length poem *The One Day*, describes the despoiling of rural New Hampshire by developers who relieve widows and widowers of ancestral land in order to build second homes "for executives retired from pricefixing for General Electric"; he might just as easily be writing about Maine, or Vermont, or rural-becoming-suburban Massachusetts. The widower's cape — a practical, heat-conserving design, probably shingled, probably with northern cedar — is destroyed and replaced by an anomalous extravaganza built in a style — and with materials — not native to any place. What had been productive pasture is paved for quick, one-time profit; never again will the land produce, lie fallow, and grow again in endless fruitful cycle, its white clover.

As for the poor, "Drag the trailer . . . / . . . to the dump: Let the poor move into the spareroom / of their town cousins." Whenever I pass the mammoth house by the side of the road, I wonder who could possibly afford to live in it. Surely not the roofer, or his son, or the landscaper's daughter. The house is useless to all but — one percent? one half percent? — of the local population; useless to the people who built it because it cannot shelter them. Like land permanently removed from food production, this lot has been removed irrevocably from the stock of liveable housing. Like the "colonial ranch" in *The One Day*, the new house that replaces the farmstead seems an emblem of labor gone awry, and work done wrong.

Work — both physical labor and the work of writing well — has always been an important subject for Donald Hall. These

two kinds of work have often been linked. In poems like "Stone
Walls" and "Great Day in the Cows' House," as well as in the
verse play *The Bone Ring*, the gift of language offered to the poet
by his grandfather is consistently paired with the gift of work.
Wesley Wells recited his poems and stories not at his leisure but
while accomplishing the tasks of a working family farm:

> He had high cheekbones, and laughed as he hoed,
> practicing his stories.

and

> While he milked he told about drummers and base-ball,
> he recited Lyceum poems about drunk deacons....

During the ideal day described in the seventh chapter of
String Too Short to Be Saved, the hours of writing poetry and
the hours of useful physical labor run seamlessly together. And
The One Day begins with a mother's bedtime story that joins
first experiences of language to a dream of work—building a
house:

> Once a little boy, and his sister—my mother lay
> on top of the quilt, narrow and tense, whispering—
> found boards piled up, deep in the woods, and nails,
> and built a house for themselves....

It is not surprising that a man of letters who has published ten
books of poems (and who has written drama, essays, criticism,
textbooks, children's books, biography, short stories, and edited
several major anthologies) finds work as important a term as
love in Freud's equation for healthy adult life. Throughout *The
One Day*, work is love's partner in the journey towards individual
identity and wholeness:

>   . . . Our longing
>   for being, beyond doubt and skepticism, assembles itself
>   from moments when the farmer scything alfalfa fills
>   with happiness as the underground cave fills with water
>   or when we lose self in the hourless hour of love.

But the "hourless hour of love" may describe the "adventure and danger" of casual adultery rather than genuine passion, and work may deteriorate into a stressful and spirit-killing grind. Work without love, in fact, paves the road to work's hell. Two characters in *The One Day* are intimates of that hell, and help define the nature of false work — as different from the true work of the farmer scything alfalfa or the sculptor in her atelier who quotes Rodin's "'. . . Work / is paradise'" as the huge colonial ranch is from the widower's cape.

The first is the speaker's father, who appears in the fourth stanza of the poem shaking his fist over his son's cradle, insisting "He'll do / what he wants to do!" Victim of a job he hates, "Bullied, found wanting," he spends twenty bitter years coming home from the lumberyard "weeping, hopeless in outrage, smoking Chesterfields, unable to sleep / for coughing. . . ." Estrangement from work one is condemned to do for twenty years engenders not only grief and rage, but death; the poem implies that the stress of work leads to a habit that will kill the father at fifty-one. No wonder he insists his son will not be enslaved by work he cannot love.

The second character who exemplifies work's hell is the widowed mother of the sculptor who will appear in *The One Day* as the speaker's female alter ego. She narrates her mother's descent into depression and alcoholism: ". . . my mother came home early from the job she hated /. . . / Sometimes she wept because she had flunked someone." Exhausted each night,

"... she collapses early with her Agatha Christie / ... with the vodka that ruptured / her liver ..." Numbed by work, she finds it difficult to respond to her daughter; they "played no more checkers" and, almost as if disaffection were contagious, the daughter stops drawing.

In each of these two cases, false work leads to rage, active or suppressed; tears; and habits that kill slowly and painfully. If this is what working wrong does to individuals, what does it do to societies?

If *The One Day*'s first section, "Shrubs Burnt Away," chronicles a series of individual hells where work, divided from love, wrecks characters like the father and mother, then the second section, "Four Classic Texts," continues this argument in terms of the *polis*. A nation, too, suffers when it is working wrong; in this case, when the making of money has been divorced from the production of useful goods.

The "Prophecy" section of "Four Classic Texts" denounces idleness and the ignorance that results from it. But it is not a lack of Yankee work ethic among today's citizens the poet means to attack; loafing, after all, has an honorable history. Rather, because we are a society both "idle / / and industrious"— destroying and subdividing perennial meadows for one-time profit; favoring the pricefixer; bulldozing the cape to raise a house no local family can afford; and believing "that money excused anything done to acquire it"— the poet locates us at the center of work's hell.

This is explicit in the "Pastoral" section of "Four Classic Texts": I argue that both its position and political concerns are central to *The One Day*. The section is structured as a dialogue between Phyllis and Marc, contemporary nymph and shepherd. Throughout, the poet uses the first and second person, especially the second person singular and first person plural. Thus, the reader seems to be included in these addresses to a "you" or a "we," and accused in the litany of working skills lost and replaced with rituals of committee meeting and country club. "You couldn't balance food and clothing on your head," says Marc to his nymph; "You practice / smiling; you forget how to milk a goat." Phyllis answers:

> You couldn't kill a rat with your putter
> even if the rat shuddered in your daughter's crib.
> You never braided rugs in your hut for the beaked ships

Instead, "You smile, you josh, you are friendly with everyone."

What sort of work do we value over husbandry and weaving? Marc: "... my manager clearcuts / the forest and paves the garden; your broker ploughs / hillsides and destroys millenial loam...." This is false work, done for quick profit, without the thought or care a farmer must give to his field of alfalfa if he intends to scythe another crop. Insidiously, "We forget / every skill we acquired over ten-thousand years of labor," in favor of learning to turn up the thermostat on our central heating, or pushing the button on a hairdryer. Why preserve land, or the skills needed to farm it, when we prefer to " ... eat non-biodegradable doughnuts and drink / whitened coffee without protest"?

Working wrong robs even the executive of his satisfaction; the manager cannot enjoy his material wealth, but confesses, " ... Ingratiating to boss and cruel / to employees, I endure my days without pleasure or purpose." Public choices — acceptance of the acquisition of money without production of liveable houses, arable soil, or useful goods, like rugs — leads to private grief.

A house is the place where public and private worlds meet. Family home, it is also the "household" numbered by census taker and tax collector; in common law it is a castle but by town law I need permission to alter it. Throughout *The One Day*, Donald Hall makes building a house a metaphor for useful work, from the dream-house of the opening stanza to the house with two chimneys in the poem's final section. Working well involves remembering " . . . how to construct aqueduct, temple, and cloaca" and eschewing the bulldozer. Let the cape, the hut, the farmhouse stand, but not the colonial ranch, symbol of work done wrong with an eye only to profit.

Meanwhile, the house by the side of the road has a "For Sale" sign in front; I watch the meadow, usually home to a dozen cows, for the surveyor's bright, brittle flags.

THE LENORE MARSHALL PRIZE

ややや   Robert Pinsky   やや

The judges for the Lenore Marshall Prize selected Donald
Hall's *The Happy Man* unanimously, from among nearly 200
books published in 1986. This book is the ninth collection of
poetry by a remarkable American writer whose first volume,
Exiles and Marriages, won the Lamont Prize thirty-two years ago.

Hall is a member of the large, diverse group of gifted American poets born around 1928, an impressive list that includes
James Merrill and Allen Ginsberg, Adrienne Rich and Phillip
Levine, John Ashbery and James Wright, Richard Howard
and Frank O'Hara, John Hollander and Anne Sexton. As my
arbitrary examples suggest, the group is as hard to generalize
about as it is distinguished. What these strong individuals
seem to share is that they became poets in the postwar years
when the triumphs of the Frost-Pound-Eliot-Stevens generation
were clear and complete. Their various, distinct individuality
could be seen as expressing the freedom or need to revise those
modernist triumphs, or turn them inside out. Hall, in his
rhythms and in his deliberate tuning down of the New England
landscape, away from extremes of transcendence and despair
and toward something like a contemporary domestic scale,
sometimes seems in loving dialectic with Frost.

That is one way to approach the particular eloquence of *The
Happy Man* and its characteristic, penetrating emotion: the feeling that happiness is relative and must inhere in daily life along

Reprinted from *The Nation*, by permission of the editor. Copyright
© 1987 *The Nation*.

with pain and labor, or else nowhere. This is a silvery, shadowed
and qualified emotional terrain, and Hall's art is to give it size,
weight and immediacy, beginning with the first images of the
first poem, "Great Day in the Cows' House":

> In the dark tie-up seven huge Holsteins
> lower their heads to feed, chained loosely to old saplings
> with whitewashed bark still on them.
> They are long dead; they survive, in the great day
> that cancels the successiveness of creatures.
> Now she stretches her wrinkly neck, her turnip-eye
> rolls in her skull, she sucks up breath . . . .

These lines celebrate the mystery inside what is partial and quotidian rather than absolute and extraordinary, with the oblique,
contradictory celebration of things and movements: we see in
the dark; the saplings are old, though saplings, but they retain
their bark; the animals are chained, but loosely; they are "dead,"
but "they survive," just as turnip-eye sounds both dead and
insistently alive. And this qualified, midway quality of the things
permeates the movement, too, as it shifts from the particular
huge animals and their highly specified tie-up to the self-
amending generalities and abstractions of the second sentence,
abstractions that tap their way through semicolon and comma.
Then the third sentence returns to the particular — Now and
she — more specified and vital than ever, but with the odor of
limitation and canceling death over all. The language itself sheds
a sad comic glow in which all things must acknowledge that they are also something else, the accepting humor
of the stoic: "Moos of revenant cattle/shake ancient timbers
and timbers still damp with sap."

   The first section of The Happy Man embodies the book's
theme in the relentless cycles of farm life, the New Hampshire

stringencies Hall has written about in his classic prose memoir *String Too Short to Be Saved*. New England seasons and habits, shifts of survival and decay, present the measured, surprisingly generous grounds for life. The second section of the volume is more direct and personal, presenting the same sense of things in a single narrative and meditative poem, "Shrubs Burnt Away," actually the free-standing first third of a projected longer work.

This poem makes explicit the world of contemporary social concerns and histories, from world war to the All-Nite-Laundro-Mart, the kind of experience that implicitly colors the bucolic material of the first section. At first, the theme seems merely to be failure and pathos. A man works at a lumberyard job he hates, "bullied, found wanting," and drives home weeping to shake his fist over his infant's cradle, with the ironic, futile words "He'll do/what he wants to do!" A gifted young woman loses track of her painting in family obligations. A marriage fails. But against or in this chain of narrative, potentially the stuff of TV serials, Hall's lines establish the quiet but nearly manic relish for life that makes us desire to live through our quite possibly calamitous episodes.

That relish is represented in the poem by the act of building, the inward act that constructs the cozy, flawed house of ourselves that we make by living:

> At the exact millisecond when two cells fused
> and multiplied, I started this house. Through years
> of milk and potty I constructed foundations. In Miss Ford's
> classroom I built it; in vacant lots hopeless at football,
> by Blake's Pond hunting for frogs and turtles,
> under the leaf's breath, in rotted leaves I built it;

in months at the worktable assembling model airplanes,
at the blackboard doing sums, in blue summer
painting watercolors at my grandmother's I built this house.
I build it now, staring at the wrist-knuckle.

This is not optimism, exactly, but rather whatever human tone
it is that turns the word "hopeless" into something affectionate,
and a little Whitmanian, in "hopeless at football." In his in-
sightful review of *The Happy Man* for *Poetry*, David Shapiro
refers to Hall's "elegy to the world without marvels" and "poetics
of imperfection." These phrases aptly characterize the child in
this poem when she visits the place her father rents when the
family breaks up: "She whirled among cheap furniture,/over
bare linoleum, saying, 'Cozy, cozy....'" The poem itself is
neither cozy nor hopeless, but able to include both terms.

Such description, and quotation from a long poem, may suggest a monochromatic, somber book. In fact, the judges were
attracted by the variety of poetry and life Hall finds within his
subject. Here is all of a short poem, one that stacks its phrases
and clauses into free-verse lines with an imitative comic
ebullience:

COUPLET
Old Timer's Day, Fenway Park, 1 May 1982

When the tall puffy
figure wearing number
nine starts
late for the fly ball,
laboring forward
like a lame truckhorse
startled by a garter snake,

> —this old fellow
> whose body we remember
> as sleek and nervous
> as a filly's—
>
> and barely catches it
> in his glove's
> tip, we rise
> and applaud weeping:
> On a green field
> we observe the ruin
> of even the bravest
> body, as Odysseus
> wept to glimpse
> among shades the shadow
> of Achilles.

The comic but respectful attitude is deftly sketched by poetry's formal joke on itself, the Ogden Nash prolongation of syntax and rhyme. It is a formal means played against the classical restraint of "we observe the ruin," the resurrection of "brave" in its old original sense of "splendid" as well as "courageous." This formal holding back while piling up generates a feeling like the significant absence of the word "Heroic" before "Couplet" in the title. In some other work, Ted Williams might be heroic; in this one, not even Achilles necessarily is. In an emotion more familiar and available than tragedy, the spectators applaud as well as weep; they are feeling a sad truth, and having a good time.

In some ways the most impressively lyrical part of this richly textured book is the concluding section, "Sisters," which takes for its keynote the word "repose." In the poem "A Sister on the Tracks" a woman walking along the railroad tracks has a nearly mystical vision of past and future linked by the ladder-like steel rails and ties, endings and beginnings on the same unbroken line, resolved by a recurrence of the image of life as a house: "Here love builds/its mortal house, where today's wind carries/a double scent of heaven and cut hay." In "A Sister by the Pond" the same character has a vision that seems more transcendent, wanting her soul to "withdraw as a fish into water . . . or into weeds that waver in water." This finality or transcendence is balanced by the concluding poem of the book, and *The Happy Man*'s final lines, which return faithfuly to the volume's chosen source, the miraculously inexhaustible source of the quotidian:

> I offer this cup to you: Though we drink
> from this cup every day, we will never drink it dry.

MORE ON
THE LENORE MARSHALL PRIZE

Ellen Bryant Voigt

Judges' panels — which is to say, three poets in one room — tend to be disputatious. This term is a synonym for "eclectic," which is to say no two judges share the same definition of, for example, *poetry*, or, for example, *excellence*.

The panel for this year's Lenore Marshall/Nation Prize was admirably eclectic. We had our views. One judge championed a group of loose-limbed, long-lined lush poems that dramatize the cycles of the natural world and man's relationship to them. The second judge preferred a more contemporary subject matter, a more urban and transitory questioning of values — in particular, a long, exploratory poem that uses fictional technique to distance autobiography or confession. The third judge did not so much arbitrate as contradict, praising a sequence of short, short-lined traditional lyrics — quiet, moving, impeccably controlled.

Happily, all of these good poems are in the same book: Donald Hall's *The Happy Man*. And that range of accomplishment is celebrated by this award.

"Range" is a word that comes to mind immediately in connection with Donald Hall. He has written about baseball, roosters, split infinitives and Ezra Pound. He has written plays, short stories, essays, biography, textbooks, columns and lectures. Before he was a man of letters, however, Donald Hall was a poet, publishing his first book of poems, *Exiles and Marriages*, at age 27, to a measure of acclaim most American poets are spared in their lifetimes.

Remarkably, this early notable promise was not a note from which the later work descends. One of the most discouraging lessons suggested by literary history is that poetry favors youth and a technical brilliance impossible to sustain. This notion gained ground through 19th century illness and accident, through 20th century madness and suicide. But Hall is writing better than ever: *The Happy Man* both extends his extraordinary elegiac volume of 1978, *Kicking the Leaves*, and anticipates the completed triptych, *The One Day*, which is ready for publication.

The deepening of resonance and power in all three of these volumes is not only a great pleasure to witness but greatly instructive. Hall has been on the lonely side of the desk before—as a teacher for many years at the University of Michigan, through his widely-adopted classroom text, *Writing Well*, in his forthright articulate criticism, and in his prescient poetry anthologies. But at the same time he has never ceased to go to school to his craft. *The Happy Man* is dedicated to 18 other writers to whom he submitted drafts of his work for rigorous criticism, before and after which he excoriated it on his own.

These are the salient facts of a lifetime in poetry—but the actual grounds for the award may be found on the pages of *The Happy Man*, where the lifetime is embodied, where technique serves moral vision.

I would like to steal outright what Donald Hall has written about Seamus Heaney:

> For all the qualities (we) list, the most important
> is song, the tune (Hall) sings which is poetry's
> tune, resolutions of cherished language.

With Robert Pack *(left)*, and Louis Simpson *(right)* during the editorial process for *The Poets of England and America*, 1956

With Mary Bly *(left)*, and James Wright *(center)* at a poetry conference at Thomas Jefferson College in Michigan, late sixties

With Deta Galloway *(left)*, and Etheridge Knight *(right)* on the occasion of a reading by Hall and Knight at the Library of Congress, 1986

Robert Bly *(left)* and Donald Hall on the platform at Hobart and William Smith Colleges, Geneva, New York, 1981

In the classroom, 1984

In Hall's room at Christ Church College, Oxford University, on the occasion of his winning the Newdigate Prize, 1952

Donald Hall in his home office at Eagle Pond Farm, 1984

REVIEWS

FROM INTENTIONS AND COMMITMENTS

❧ Winfield Townley Scott ❧

To the Loud Wind and Other Poems, 1955

Since reviewers of poetry are recruited from those who care about poetry it seems necessarily to follow in these stringent times that the reviewers more often than not are also themselves writers of poetry. I think this is frequently unfortunate. At the same time I confess I cannot suggest a less personal system of reviewing that would be fool-proof. It is unlikely, for instance, that we could be greatly illuminated if all poetry reviewing were in the hands of nonproductive academicians.

A young poet may bring a valuable freshness to such reviewing because he is young and therefore, almost always, himself unformed as a poet. But when those of us who continue writing poetry move into middle age we are bound to have arrived by talents and limitations at prejudices of poetry; for better, for worse, for success or failure, each goes his own way. Out of our mature prejudices we may then speak freshly of poets among the dead or among our elders; I think we are not likely to say anything of much value about our contemporaries or to be alert spotters of talent among the youngsters. I do not say — hopefully, I would not say — that the poet in his mid-forties is fixed, is set; it is simply, absorbed in the ways he has found for attempting poetry, how can he bring a proper critical absorption to the work of others around him? He cannot. By the nature of what

he is doing he has become a lifelong defendant and therefore —
well, not disqualified as a judge but at least to be held in suspicion as a special pleader.

Donald Hall's pamphlet shows evidence of this instinct; indeed
of conviction — he says "I bury the cheap magic that I know."
He has a tiny poem (if a good poem is ever tiny, which I doubt)
on marriage which, for all its different level of experience, has
the brazen simplicity of Stevenson in A Child's Garden of Verses.
Hall's tendency appears to be not merely the direct statement
but the didactic. His poem "The Tree" is a good example, and
his several epigrams reveal he has humor at his side. I pause
for one sample which I hope will not be out of place here:

> I learned in a vision a secret that nobody knows:
> Criticism must be at least as well-written as prose.

FROM FIVE POINTS OF THE COMPASS

Stanley Kunitz

Exiles and Marriages, 1955

These five volumes in hand, four of them first collections, have little in common with one another, and I shall not pretend that they have, though it is always a temptation in an omnibus review to facilitate comparison by inventing for the occasion a schematic unity that will at least serve to demonstrate the superiority of the critical intelligence to the wayward enterprise of the subject poets, whose vaunted intuition should have prepared them for being manipulated as counters in somebody else's ingenious game of hypotheses and values. As for the diversity itself, one might adduce it as evidence of the atomization of the world of modern poetry, its failure to achieve a consistent pattern, signified by so much lonely running in search of a language and a theme; or, conversely, as evidence of the independence of spirit and wholesome variety charactristic of a flourishing literary economy. The one general remark I feel inclined to make is almost embarrassingly simple: each of these poets, in at least some of his work, has given me the kind of pleasure that I associate with the reading of good poetry. Invariably the poets who are easiest to discuss are those whose intentions are most readily defined—and that is why I began by talking about John Logan and Donald Hall....

For a first book, or indeed for almost any book of poems,

Donald Hall's *Exiles and Marriages* has been published with considerable *éclat*. It was honored before publication as the 1955 Lamont Poetry Selection of the Academy of American Poets — aimed at furthering "the discovery and encouragement of new poetic genius" — , has received unusually prompt and flattering attention in the press, and has even been nominated (unofficially, of course) by *Time* for the Pulitzer Prize. So far as I have been able to observe, the other poets that I am reviewing here have received the laggard and fairly perfunctory kind of notice that is the usual fate of the American poet. Why this discrepancy? It might be said that Donald Hall is cleverer than the others, having already gotten on record his jibes at the poet Finesse,

> Who writes his verse in order to amaze,
> To win the Pulitzer, or *Time's* sweetest praise;
> Who will endure a moment, and then pass,
> As hopeless as an olive in his glass.

May I inquire, however, why that martini olive is described as "hopeless?" None in my extensive acquaintance has ever seemed so to me.

Perhaps this poet has the good fortune, in his *persona*, to be blest with the common American touch, whatever that may be, which makes it possible to single him out from his contemporaries. I wonder who else among them, if "exiled" to Oxford, would publicly hanker for a good old New England Thanksgiving dinner,

> Where turkey roasted whole,
> Potatoes, turnips, peas,
> Onions and Brussels sprouts,
> And globes of Holland cheese,

> Where pumpkin, apple, mince,
> And seven kinds of pie,
> Plum pudding, cake, and nuts
> Astound and satisfy.

If it is profundity one seeks, one can, if one will, chew on such sentences as,

> There's no security except the grave;
> There's much belief in what does not exist,

or on these, in a more lyric vein:

> The young are never robbed of innocence
> But given gold of love and memory.
> We live in wealth whose bounds exceed our sense,
> And when we die are full of memory.

If we admire Auden, we can find much to remind us of him, and if we love Yeats, we can perhaps enjoy the sportive query,

> When that sweet action is at last unloosed,
> How can you tell seducer from seduced?

The jacket tells us that these poems "are subtle and often provocatively strange, but always written with precision and complete clarity. They are personal but not private — they communicate." Often what they seem to be communicating beyond all else is their desire to communicate. We expect a poet now and then to announce his art and his hope for immortality, but if the stance becomes too familiar it begins to affect us like a piece of outmoded statuary around the house. The modern poet, we are told, is too introverted and costive, but one of the troubles with this collection of a young man of twenty-seven is that there is just too much of it, over sixty poems, some of which seem to have leaped straight into print from his scrapbooks.

I do not mean to imply that Donald Hall is a poet without talent or accomplishment. Though his poems are unremarkable for sensibility or texture, he can write a clean line in conventional stress, and he can build a structure, command an action. The energy of his will is such that at times it seems to be usurping the role of imagination, but at least it can be said that none of the poems falters through psychic fatigue or inertia. Granted that the genre is no longer a novelty, he had made brilliant use on occasion of current pseudo-mythic materials, as in "Matter of Fact," "Cops and Robbers," and "The Body Politic":

> I never thought until I pulled the trigger
> But that I did the difficult and good.
> I thought republics stood for something bigger,
> For the mind of man, as Plato said they stood.

Hall's Newdigate Prize Poem, "Exile," is one of his best. Other poems that I like are "The Strangers," "At Delphi," "The Sleeping Giant," "Jamaica" (a promising departure in its linguistic density), "Wedding Party," and "Syllables of a Small Fig Tree," which charms me because it is so unassuming:

> I am dead, to be sure,
> for thwarting Christ's pleasure,
> Jesus Christ called Saviour.
>
> I was a small fig tree.
> Unjust it seems to me
> that I should withered be.
>
> If justice sits with God,
> Christ is cruel Herod
> and I by magic dead.
>
> If there is no justice
> where great Jehovah is,
> I will the devil kiss.

I wish there were more of that air of intimacy in Hall's work. (Not sentimentality, which is an enemy of intimacy and which bubbles in several of his "personal" poems.) In one of his letters Yeats referred to intimacy as "the mark of fine literature." To it he opposed generalization. "And generalization," he wrote, "creates rhetoric, wins immediate popularity, organizes the mass, gives political success, Kipling's poetry, Macaulay's essays and so on. . . . Generalization meets one in music-hall songs with their mechanical rhythm, or in thoughts taken from the newspapers." The text seems to me pertinent.

TIME'S SWEET PRAISE

శ్రీ *Time* Magazine ∾

Exiles and Marriages, 1955

Now, as always, poets are a dime a dozen and good poetry is very hard to come by. The sad fact is that the best poets now alive are also among the oldest (T.S. Eliot, Robert Frost, e.e. cummings), and they are not adding significantly to their output. So when a young one comes along who has poet written all over him, the literary weather improves distinctly.

Poet Donald Hall, 27, has not yet unseated the great oldsters, but with his very first book, he has made a solid seat for himself. *Exiles and Marriages* has neither the poetic blaze of Dylan Thomas nor the suppressed smolder of Robert Frost, but it has its own true tone composed in almost equal parts of intelligence and imagination. Like most good poets, Hall knows that

Life is hell, but death is worse.

And it is possible that even in an age of anxiety he puts on the hair shirt of guilt more often than is strictly necessary ("I wear — inside — the horizontal stripe"). But Poet Hall is very much alive, and alive to many things. He sings with grace in praise of his native New Hampshire, and he can celebrate his marriage and the birth of his son without seeming mawkish or losing a shred of dignity. A visit to Delphi is fastened into his experience with this finality:

> No priestess spoke. I heard one sound.
> The donkey's sure and nerveless plod
> Past ruined columns of a god
> Made dactyls on the ground.

And he can also show himself to be a thoughtful man and poet of his time:

> I name an age of choice and discontent
> Whose emblem is "the difficult to choose."
> Each man is free to act, but his intent
> Must circumscribe what he may not refuse.
> Each moment is political, and we
> Are clothed in nothing but mortality.

Harvard-and-Oxfordman Hall has won prizes for his poems both here and in England. He has deserved them. In "Six Poets in Search of a Lawyer," Hall loftily disparages the sort of poet

> Who writes his verse in order to amaze,
> To win the Pulitzer, or TIME's *sweet praise.*

But the fact is that if he goes on writing, he is almost a cinch to win both.

ON *EXILES AND MARRIAGES*

William Arrowsmith

Exiles and Marriages, 1955

My over-all impression of Mr. Donald Hall's *Exiles and Marriages* is one of a general level of competence so high that it almost obscures the fact that this volume contains an alarmingly high percentage of poetic odd-jobs and merely fashionable exercises. The knack of verse he certainly has, a knack particularly conspicuous in his professional handling of line and rhyme and the impression of good competence everywhere well sustained. His given form is, like Simpson's, the traditional verse period, aided by a clever and inventive ear; but Mr. Hall nowhere experiments or takes risks with his form, being evidently content to work with the given, except for a little artful roughening here and there and an adroit use of part-lines. The result is a compact tidiness of feeling, with the deliberate tracing of rough edges to indicate an illusion of passion (passion seems to me almost completely absent); there is a mellowness of statement, putative and gently aphoristic, though at times the mellowness becomes almost as mechanical as the form; and there is a calmness and smoothness coming close to blandness in both form and statement, as though Mr. Hall were an old man, in deep control of dead experience, and nowhere capable of surprise. But he writes well, and if we recognize the Yeats or Auden who give him a form that is not his own or a wisdom before

First published in *The Hudson Review*, Vol. IX, No. 2 (Summer, 1956). Reprinted by permission of the author. Copyright © 1956 William Arrowsmith.

his time, this does not annul the sense of talent or put him outside promise. There is both promise and professional competence in poetry like this:

> No man can knock his human fist upon
> The door built by his mind, or hear the voice
> He meditated come again if gone;
> We live outside the country of our choice.
> Leaning toward harvest, fullness as our end,
> Our habits will not mend.
> Our humanness betrays us to the cage
> Within whose limits each is free to walk,
> But where no man can hear our prayers or rage,
> And none of us can break the walls to talk.

Opposed to the promise, I think, is Mr. Hall's own penchant for a professionalism that is so smooth at times that it comes close to dishonesty or to competent hackwork (see the lazy, attitudinizing elegy called "An Elegy for Wesley Wells," or the empty competence of "Carol," or the trite artificiality of "Epigenethlion"). This professionalism is further troubled by a kind of gentlemanliness and well-bred mannerizing whose difficulties are not that they are poses but that Mr. Hall cannot shake much poetry out of them: most of what Mr. Hall's gentlemanliness comes to is a sort of social kindliness and solid decency and even a cloying muffling softness with ideas and passions. The softness with ideas is particularly noticeable, and accounts, I think, for the blurring effect of some of his less earned *sententiae*; intellectual rigor and power are, even less than passion, a part of Mr. Hall's initial poetic gifts. And lacking these, or failing to devleop them, he turns quite naturally to the perfection of his human skills, or those human skills which are best earned in the gentler regions of social life — compassion,

fellow-feeling, friendliness, regret, grace in growing old and staying young. These gentler and humbler skills are, it is true, not
altogether accepted by Mr. Hall, who now and again announces
his intention to have a *Sturm und Drang* and give the bastinado
with his tongue; but as yet this is only a fetching braggadocio
from a poet with a domesticated Muse. At the moment, Mr.
Hall's apparent subject is less a subject than a habitual attitude,
but this attitude is in striking harmony with his chosen form;
if there is to be development, it will need to come in taking
a purchase in greater risk of strong feeling and beginning from
formal scratch anew. In the meantime, Mr. Hall's competence
makes an entertaining and handsome first book.

FROM A WORD FROM THE SCULLERY

Anthony Hecht

The Dark Houses, 1958

The readers and the hearers like my books,
But yet some writers cannot them digest.
But what care I? For when I make a feast,
I would my guests should praise it, not the cooks.

—Sir John Harrington, 1618

When the powers that play upon our lives seem unusually vast and inhuman; when values have their authority only under limited and freely exchangeable visions of life; when individuals are desperate to discover their identities and have no clue but statistics; then impudence is taken for courage, and irreverence for manly independence. It is true that nobody walks down our streets leading a live lobster on a leash of pink ribbon, but our tastes for this sort of thing are still active. Enid Starkie was writing in 1944 about the eccentrics of the eighteen-thirties, and Dr. Edith Sitwell has just given us a book on the English eccentrics. *Auntie Mame* is a smash hit, and, in another way, so is *Howl*. It is liberating even to be able to admire these free spirits; and what if it could be shown that what seems like their naughtiness is really, paradoxically, a sign of their goodness? So that Baudelaire might be restored to the very bosom of the church, and might presently become the patron saint of blasphemers. Clearly those innocent emancipators who started out mainly to shock the bourgeois had got hold of something more powerful and complex than they realized. A lover's ruthless indifference to the feelings of the women he seduces is a sign that he is one of the few who have that energetic potency and demanding vitality that would make him sexually attractive: his ultimate indifference proves his insatiability, his overmastering virility. Let thieves, perverts and idlers be our heroes, then, for they are "honest" men who will not be coerced by the trumped-up conventions of society. By these lights, any assault on what passes for good taste is a blow struck for freedom; and deliberate vulgarity becomes an admirable way of life. When this can be done with both humor and compassion, we may have great works like *Moll Flanders* and *The Beggar's Opera*. When the compassion is missing we may still have the witty, though sometimes pointless, epigrams of Oscar Wilde. Now, inverted pieties can become a chic and easy way of dealing with the world; yet who is to say at what point this famous posture loses its human shape? Who, I mean, can say this without sounding like a narrow moralist?

Donald Hall's first book was the Lamont Poetry Selection for 1955, and was generously praised everywhere. It was a book of great charm and wit, its assurance and amusement always apparent. The present volume in comparison might be thought solemn. It is, rather, a superbly brave attempt not to repeat the triumph of the first book but to try for something even more difficult: a steady and appraising vision which is earned in art as in life only at great cost. It can be said of him that in trying to keep his balance about difficult subjects he sometimes attains to flatness; and this seems to me true of the elegy for his father. It can also be said that a poem called "The Family" is one of the most carefully horrifying poems to have been written in some time time. The work for this book is not "earnest," though "free spirits" might regard it as such: earthbound, concerned. And those "free spirits" could undoubtedly show that my tastes were those of a moralist.

FROM POETRY AS WRITTEN

❦ Thom Gunn ❦

The Dark Houses, 1958

I suppose Pound's remark that poetry should be as well written as prose has become pretty well worked by now, though it has been taken seriously by few writers, even among his contemporaries. Yet it is still an epigram that every poet ought to write at the start of every new notebook. What it suggests is that we should apply to poetry the same rigorous standards of clear English as to good prose, e.g. that we should refrain from irrelevance and support all our general statements. And after this the poet should perhaps write a short prayer that he be not captivated by his own public character and thus forget that he is "saying something" quite as much as the novelist or dramatist or essayist. The sad fact is that six of these nine books are far less competently written than various modern novels that I have read lately; and at least three of these six do not contain poems as direct or as witty or as energetic as the best songs on the juke box of the bar next door. I say this, not in contempt of poetry, but in the knowledge that poetry is, today as at any time, potentially the greatest of the written arts. . . .

In his second book, *The Dark Houses,* Donald Hall makes a deliberate effort to extend his range in subject matter and technique, in the latter more successfully than in the former.

Clearly the book is not a mere random collection of the poems
he has written in the last few years. The first section especially,
"Houses on Residential Streets," has been conceived as a unity:
its subject is the loneliness and lack of given values in the
bourgeoisie. Most of it is accurate and well put but has a certain
obviousness. Hall's attitude to his subject is complex, a mix-
ture of identification and outsiderishness, of sympathy and
exasperation, but one feels a thinness in most of the poems in
this section. The best of them is "The Foundations of American
Industry"—which starts like a piece of imagism but ends as far
more, reminding me in structure of some of the poems in
Harmonium; but more typical of the group is "The Widows,"
of which I quote the first and last stanzas.

> Up and down the small streets, in which
> no two houses are exactly
> alike, widows of all ages
> sit alone playing solitaire,
> or knitting, or sometimes baking,
> left in the big, empty houses. . . .
>
> Book clubs, television, and ways
> to supplement their small incomes
> keep them busy. It is not a
> bad life, they say, for there are so
> many left like you, though no two
> widows are exactly alike.

Though the end gives the poem a very neat turn, I wonder
whether the poet has really said more than, say, Terence Rattigan
in *Separate Tables* (of course he avoids Rattigan's sentimentality).

   The other section of the book is less unified and much more
interesting. It also deals with "Men Alone," but they are on
the whole more intelligent men than those in the first section,

there is no overlapping of theme, and there is a far greater range of tone, as one can tell from reading such excellent poems as "The Tailor," "Marat's Death," and "Sestina."

Perhaps the principal achievement of the book is in Hall's use of syllabic blank verse, two techniques by which he produces an effect where the deliberate flatness of a certain type of free verse is combined with the emotional control of regular meter. These techniques are especially appropriately managed in the "Three Poems from Edvard Munch":

> Charlotte, the will begins to
> revise you to leather. How
> volition hurts the skin of girls!
>
> Marat is dead. The people
> of France will endure his death,
> l'ami du peuple and no man.
>
> Marat had skin which boiled like
> water on a stove. His wet
> and cruel skin has one wound more.

This is only part of the second poem, "Marat's Death," which should be read in its entirety, but it demonstrates the unobtrusive intensity of his style at its best.

FROM PUZZLERS

Martin Dodsworth

A Roof of Tiger Lilies, 1963

In the Guggenheim exhibition now at the Tate Gallery there is a picture by René Magritte which is good in a way that I find puzzling. It is a large canvas and shows a housefront at night, lit by a single street-lamp whose light hardly reaches to the eaves. Above the roof, tree-tops are silhouetted black and lacy against the sky of a sunny spring day, filled with small, soft, very white clouds, and utterly unnocturnal. It is odd how much at home that sky seems with the night scene beneath, as though the artificial, paradoxical, conjunction of opposites which is the basis of the picture had been softened somehow into naturalism. It works brilliantly as a metaphor, bringing together feelings common to its two elements, whose real diversity is emphasized, however, by the use of different styles for house and sky. Unity of ideas counts for more than diversity of style. It is just here, though, that the puzzle arises: If the force of the picture lies in its idea, in what could be understood of it even before it was painted, then it is difficult to see what is contributed by *these* particular brush-strokes, by *this* suggestion of light, to the general theme. Style is so far overshadowed by initial conception that the traditional terms of criticism, which lay importance on the unique nature of the work of art and on individual interpretation, seem not to be quite applicable.

Similar kinds of puzzle arise in these three recent books of verse—not that their poems happen to be mysterious in the way their subject-matter shapes its form. This kind of mysteriousness has become not uncommon recently; the traditional formal patterns of verse favoured ten years ago have now been abandoned largely by younger poets in preference for free and syllabic forms so self-effacing that their expressive function is in doubt. Donald Hall is a poet who succeeds where many have failed, and *A Roof of Tiger Lilies* is an excellent book, but from the point of view of form and rhythm it remains mystifying. He writes with an eloquent simplicity that puts questions of metric firmly to one side; to praise him for his style would be like congratulating Pascal on his: not wrong, but largely irrelevant to the matters in hand. He does not decorate his poems; they speak for themselves with a kind of Puritan gravity and intentness, which surely owes something to their author's New Hampshire childhood.

They return again and again to the subject of death:

> Like an old man,
> whatever I touch I turn
> to the story of death.

Death is ambiguously symbolized by snow, which "must / come down, even if it struggles / to stay in the air with the strength / of the wind." It is cold, gradual, and has an absolute purity in its whiteness; it preludes the birth of the year as surely as it delays it. It gathers slowly and cannot be prevented:

> the snow keeps falling
> and something will always be falling.

In another poem we are told of the poet's father that "his early death grew inside him / like snow piling on the grass." Mr. Hall's best poems all have this note of unforced sadness.

The short lines which I have quoted suggest that though he uses great simplicity of technique it is far from unsophisticated. Death *grows* as snow *piles*; the two verbs don't really match up, and so deftly hint at the uneasiness with which death's place in the economy of life is viewed. By placing together *I touch* and *I turn* Mr. Hall suggests what was at once the gift and curse of Midas; by ending two successive lines emphatically with *falling*, he demonstrates how that word's very sound and meaning refuse to accept stress. His style is full of felicities; the likeness to Magritte lies in one's not seeing how the felicities are rooted in this way of saying things only. Each poem is a sequence of more or less simple statements which fall together — like snow — and hint at the contours of feeling beneath. One is at once satisfied and baffled by the bareness of his poems.

The shorter ones are, on the whole, noticeably less good, perhaps because they are not able to use repetition and contrast with such unostentatious cunning. They have to be more explicit, and their simplicity seems more artificial. Even the longer pieces become at times sentimental, as though Mr. Hall's tight-lipped curb on obvious feeling were too difficult to maintain. "The Old Pilot's Death," for example, is fanciful and evasive:

> In the distance, circling,
> in a beam of late sun like birds migrating,
> there are thin wings of a thousand biplanes.
> He banks and flies to join them.

This does not represent the general level of achievement; the best poems are continuously, yet mutely, surprising but right — these lines from "New Hampshire" may give an idea:

> Fat honey bees
> meander among raspberries where a quarrel
> of vines crawls into the spilled body of a plane.

The mind enters a series of shocks in reading this simple, descriptive sentence. First it is lulled by the *meandering* of the bees and then jolted awake by the *quarrel*. But the quarrel turns out to be only metaphorical — only *vines*. The vines, however, *crawl* like insects dabbling in something *spilled* (raspberry jam, perhaps; the innocence of the bees seems to be invoked here). The fact that it is a *body* that has been spilled changes one's reaction yet again; only the body of a *plane*, of course, but the human disaster, already suggested by the quarrel, effectively darkens the natural scene. These successive shocks are held in check by the syllabic line, whose irregular stresses are deployed to soften the blows as they come. Both *vines* and *crawls* are stressed yet juxtaposed — "a quarrel of *vines crawls*" — and this modifies the force with which their meaning strikes us. Mr. Hall is astonishingly good at this sort of thing; he uses syllabic verse with such skill that one neglects to ask why he chose it in the first place. But if you ask the question, it is mystifying; the poems exist suspended in mid-air, with no general context of feeling or norm of rhythm to which to refer.

ON *A ROOF OF TIGER LILIES*

Robert Mazzocco

A Roof of Tiger Lilies, 1963

In the mid-Fifties, when Henry Luce absolved certain de-
radicalized intellectuals and christened them Men of Affirmation, academic poetry shifted gears. A popular example of such
a turnabout was Donald Hall's first volume: awkwardness à la
Hardy, elegance à la Auden, a New England earnestness and
Harvard wit, *l'éducation sentimentale* the theme, and no moan-
ing at all.

> I took the stair again, and said good-by
> To childhood and return,
> Nostalgia for illusion, and the lie
> Of isolation. May I earn
> An honest eye.

In his next book, three years later, the suburbs darkened; snap-
shots of people and places expressed an uneasy mockery, or a
queasy wisdom, somewhat like Larkin's. With *A Roof of Tiger
Lilies*, style and sensibility drastically contract. The impression
is one of entering a monk's cell, where the few objects on view
seem to have come from some other place, from enormously
cluttered other rooms. A description like that, of course,
characterizes the "hermetic" poem, a European product. Yet if
Hall is quite recognizably American and still uses a mostly

syllabic structure or blank verse, the elusive transitions, the seemingly uneventful actions, suggest a foreign aura, as do the dehydrated wonder and suffering, and the solace, what there is of it, that exists primarily between the lines.

Hall's culture heroes, judging by his poems, are the artists Munch and Henry Moore, and Henry James, whose time-travel fantasy, *A Sense of the Past* (which inspired the play *Berkeley Square*), is interestingly treated in "The Beau of the Dead." But though no reference is made to it, it is another James work, *The Beast in the Jungle*—that tale of unused energies revenging themselves—which proves to be the real crux of the matter. Hall addresses himself "to the grand questions," so states the dust jacket; I think, on the contrary, he evades them. What is exhibited in these poems is not so much the inability to feel, but the diffident, dispassionate man's inaccessibility to experience, to let loose the demons. Guilt, waste, thanatophobia, a mood of suspended desperation hovers everywhere. Indeed at thirty-seven, Hall appears to be taking on the burden of approaching middle age as if he were Atlas getting ready to carry the world. Also a feeling of isolation is here, especially, I gather, from History: the recent wars which made no sense, the rumors of wars which never end. In his beautifully controlled nature studies, in the eerie impressionistic rememberance of his father, or some other aspect of his past, and in the pictures of estranged husbands and wives or lovers, some outlet is sought, some transfiguring "leap" proposed. Yet, to me, anyway, what comes across is merely a nostalgic drift, oblique emotional gestures. Psychologically, these poems do not fulfill themselves; aesthetically, however, I consider them Hall's most impressive achievement. Special, sparse, magnetic, the best of them haunt the mind, moving on a dark tide, like an ice floe down river.

It is difficult to predict what Hall will do next. Each of his volumes has grown successively more negative in tone, though always ending on a note of uplift: the glamor of human endurances in the first two, a sort of neo-mysticism here. "Birth is the fear of death," he says in the opening poem; "I am ready for the mystery," he says in the last. Among his contemporaries, his affinities are with James Wright, James Dickey, Louis Simpson, and especially, Robert Bly, the least mentioned but probably the most talented of the group.

Here is Hall's "At Thirty-Five" in part:

> But if the world is a dream
> The puffed stomach of Juan is a dream
> and the rich in Connecticut are dreaming.
>
> There are poor bachelors
> who live in shacks made of oilcans
> and broken doors, who stitch their shirts
> until the cloth disappears under stitches,
> who collect nails in tin cans.
>
> The wind is exhausted.

Here's Bly:

> The rich man in his red hat
> Cannot hear
> The weeping in the pueblos of the lily,
> Or the dark tears in the shacks of the corn.
> Each day the sea of light rises
> I hear the sad rustle of the darkened armies,
> Where each man weeps, and the plaintive
> Orisons of the stones.
> The stones bow as the saddened armies pass.

SOME NOTES ON *THE ALLIGATOR BRIDE*

William Matthews

The Alligator Bride: Poems New and Selected, 1969

In Donald Hall's early poems we are reminded that America lacks an ancient history. Henry James' lament in his book on Hawthorne is famous, probably for the wrong reasons: we don't suffer from lack of an Eton but from lack of a Stonehenge.

Instead, and since our forefathers erased whatever history the Indians might have left us, we will have to become fiercely phenomenological: we still need to look at things intensely to see if any of our past is clinging to them. Often in Hall's early poems the answer is NO.

> I walked the streets where I was born and grew,
> And all the streets were new.

The lament in these lines from "Exile" is echoed by the title "No Deposit No Return." In that poem Hall notes that in the Dordogne Paleolithic inscriptions survive, but we have trouble going farther back than Barbara Fritchie. Interestingly, this eroding past is connected in Hall's imagination to the relationship between parents and children. "My Son, My Executioner" ends like this:

> We twenty-five and twenty-two
> Who seemed to live forever,

> Observe enduring life in you
> And start to die together.

And in "The Foundation of American Industry" Hall watches the workmen from a Ford plant go home:

> when they walk home
> they walk on sidewalks
> marked W
> P A 38;
> their old men made
> them, and they walk on
> their fathers.

As if Hall sensed early (*Exiles and Marriages* and *The Dark Houses*, in which these poems from Section I of *The Alligator Bride* first appeared, were published in 1955 and 1958) where and why we would export the anxieties arising from this fearful parenticide, he wrote these lines to end "These Faces":

> I cannot see the watch on my wrist
> without knowing that I am dying,
> and that a new politician is
> being born, perhaps in Jakarta.

A poem dedicated to his father ends:

> I will go back and leave you here to stay
> Where the dark houses harden into sleep.

"Je Suis Une Table" ends:

> and there is nothing at all
> but inner silence, nothing
> to relieve on principle
> now this intense thickening.

It is as if the American psyche were, like a bonsai tree, clipped back by its lack of history from all growth but thickening. We stare longingly at old things but fear them because they represent the death our children will visit upon us. No wonder so many Americans hate the young.

Section II reprints poems from *A Roof of Tiger Lilies*, and in it Hall is not only talking of a nostalgia for old things, he is trying to experience them imaginatively. In "In the Kitchen of an Old House" he spies on the first meeting of his father and mother:

> A shout gathered inside me
>   like a wind, to break the rhythm;
> to keep him from entering
>   that door—. . .

Yet in another poem he admits that

> though the oak was the shade of old summers,
> I loved the guttural saw.

And in "The Snow":

> whatever I touch I turn
> to the story of death.

Trapped between a past built on parenticide and a future of sacrifice to children, where can the self turn? Hall writes of two alternatives that particularly interest me: one occurs in his air-crash poems; in a few poems from this period ("Digging," "Internal and External Forms," "Self-Portrait, As a Bear," and "The Wives") another begins to try to imagine a form in which it can manifest itself.

In the first of the air-crash poems, "New Hampshire," nature invades the site of a plane crash: "a quarrel / of vines crawls into the spilled body of the plane." Though the plane is down,

bees "meander among raspberries." The bees are fat, like the
bear in "Self-Portrait, As a Bear": "It is eating flowers which
makes him fat." Death is one escape from the self, abandonment another. In the poems from Section II they are so close
it is difficult to see them as different alternatives. Both step outside the relentless path travelled by the forces that inhabit the
titles of Hall's first two books. These forces are deathly: the exile
takes place in the dark house full of family: the father you must
kill, the wife you will beget children with who will kill you in
turn: worst, in one way and another, you love them all. If this
is flight, let's either have a crash or let the body continue to
fly without the plane, abandoning everything but itself and its
cargo of flowers.

In another air-crash poem, "The Old Pilot,"

> When he looks up, his propeller is turning,
> although no one was there to snap it.

This sense of being involved in a process not of his own insti-
gation fascinates Hall. Later in the same poem the old pilot "feels
the old fear, and rising over the fields / the old gratitude." It
would be fearful because it would be like one's increasingly un-
willing participation in the cycle of family and parenticide and
death. It would inspire gratitude because one hopes to escape this
cycle by events equally outside one's control: death or
abandonment.

It is interesting to compare two poems from Section III, "The
Man in the Dead Machine" and "The Blue Wing." In the first
poem—the "dead machine" is surely the engine that carries a life
relentlessly forward according to a received pattern—we first
see a pilot in World War II. Then we find he is dead, crashed,
and next:

> Or say that the shrapnel
> missed him, he flew
> back to the carrier, and every
> morning takes his chair, his pale
> hands on the black arms, and sits
> upright, held
> by the firm webbing.

In "The Blue Wing" the speaker walks in the rain bareheaded but not wet, thinking of a woman, "singing light songs / about women."

> A blue wing tilts at the edge of the sea.

> The wreck of the small
> airplane sleeps
> drifted to the high tide line,
> tangled in seaweed, green
> glass from the sea.

> The tiny skeleton inside
> remembers the falter of engines, the
> cry without
> answer, the long dying
> into
> and out of the sea.

Clearly it is better not to have made it back to the carrier: the "cry without" (what a telling enjambment!) is better than the cry within, and if a woman is involved it is possible to die not onto the land but into "and out of the sea." We first see such an idea of abandonment attached to women in "The Wives":

> If I said, "Little wives,
> shut in your dark
> houses, an enormous
> tiger lily splits
> the roof of each house . . .

Once, not having read the poem for a while and trying,
without a text handy, to describe it to a friend, I mistakenly
said it was the poem in which the houses began to breathe.
A mistake in terms of the actual text, but not in terms of its
metaphorical urgency. One thing changes as we near the later
poems: at first the wives are seen from a long distance, "little,"
but later things begin to be life-size.

There is still the fear of stiffening to death: in "The Grave,
The Well":

> Women are leaning back in taxis.
> Men stoop into taxis
> after them, and enter the
> grave, the well, the mine
> of fur and scent.

Or in a poem about mens' rooms,

> I have felt the sadness
> of the small white tiles,
> the repeated shapes
> and the unavoidable whiteness.

Earlier in Hall's life as a poet he would have stopped there,
knowing which phenonmenon to meditate on but unable to
imagine a first thought about it. But now he goes on:

> They are my uncles,
> these old men
> who are only plumbing,
> who throb with tears all night
> and doze in the morning.

Even in these later poems Hall can't see the old things he
missed in his earliest poems: rather he is able to look at newer
things and see them originally (see their origins). In the New

World we have always had to imagine a link with the rest of the world—didn't we purposefully cut the links that were easy to see? And it will be necessary to imagine in the present a future that can survive the guttural saw. Thus in the poem "Gold" Hall celebrates a gold and yellow room—picking "gold" for a title redeems the mining metaphor at the end of "The Well, The Grave"—in which the poem's speaker has spent happy hours with a beloved woman.

> We made in those days
> tiny identical rooms inside our bodies
> which the men who uncover our graves
> will find in a thousand years
> shining and whole.

And in "Lovers in Middle Age" what is old—a woman's face in contrast to the unlined faces of college students also waiting in line at a movie—is both accessible and valuable. The poem ends:

> Today we made love all day.
> I look at you. You are smiling at the sidewalk,
> dear wrinkled face.

In an early poem sidewalks were the fathers of the workers at the Ford plant in Ypsilanti. In "The Wives" the speaker goes on—after speaking of tiger lilies splitting the roofs of the dark houses—, goes on to tell the wives that he had seen such a thing only in a dream and that they will be so disappointed not to live the dream that they will walk by themselves

> for a long time
> on the white sidewalks.

In this poem the whiteness of the sidewalks is like the long-gone but still reflected promise of marriage, whose ceremonies are obsessed by whiteness as a symbol of nothing having happened yet: happiness as the absence of event. In "Lovers in Middle Age" the woman can smile at the sidewalk.

Both "Gold" and "Lovers in Middle Age" will be reprinted in Hall's forthcoming book, now in manuscript, *The Yellow Room: Love Poems*. The link between Section III of *The Alligator Bride* and the new manuscript is interesting because we see that, as Hall's vision focuses itself so narrowly as to provide us with an entire book of love poems, it at the same time brings together his lifelong themes of abandonment, old things, the cry without, the fear of death by stiffening, the air-crash and love.

The language in the poems I like best is so simple it would be boring if the poems were not so usefully informed by obsession. In this respect *The Alligator Bride* is like a funnel. The earlier poems have been revised most extensively (and it is interesting to compare the current texts to their first published versions) and are, still, the most rhetorical. Nearing the end of the book, the poems become on their surfaces translucent and simple: we see what is beneath their surfaces. In a few places there is nothing there: the poem about mens' rooms, for example, partakes of a new rhetoric of apparent simplicity which in this poem turns out to be a linguistic rather than a spiritual simplicity. If it were not for the interesting place the poem holds in Hall's development we would not long be interested by it.

Often, though, the poems toward the end of the book pass through the narrow neck and splay out again, fuller than we would know them to be if we read them singly. I think of one tiny lovely poem in *The Yellow Room: Love Poems*. If we think of the search in the new world for origins and the ambiguity such a search provides in our lives, if we think of the fierce urge Hall's poems have to give themselves over to something outside the self trapped by that ambiguity, if we think of the imaginative distance he has travelled, the poem shows openly its value and cost:

> Generous tiny hands,
> never go back
> to your old country.

POETS IN VARYING DEGREES

Robert Stock

The Yellow Room: Love Poems, 1971

I wish I could call Donald Hall's new book blinding in its intensity and insight; I wish I could call it moving or even interesting;
and, on the other hand, I wish I could say that his work has
run downhill since he abandoned "Neo-Augustinism" for
whatever he is up to now. Alas, Mr. Hall has perhaps improved; alas, he has not improved enough to matter. *The Yellow
Room* is in the tradition of a series of poems charting the seas
(usually rough) of a love affair (usually illicit). Perhaps we think
of the Roman elegiac poets or the Renaissance sonnet sequences,
or John Berryman's recent revival of the tradition in his own
sonnet sequence, followed by Shapiro's *The White-Haired Lover.*
But in Donald Hall's collection, the focus slips. The object of
the poet's attention is no longer the beloved, nor is it the affair
(a skimpy one as presented), nor is it even the lover, who is as
a man a sentimental solipsist and, as a poet, a chameleon gone
mad on scraps of plaid. Indeed his whole iconography is out
of focus. Take his imagery of rooms, for example, an obsession
since his first book. A habitual mode of Hall's is the symbol
of outer and inner rooms. "New Room," in the present book,
attempts this movement; but the transitions, like the separate
poems in the book, run into one another like Silly Putty, losing all sense of rooms. Another instance of slipped focus occurs

Reprinted from *The Nation,* by permission of the editor. Copyright
© 1971 *The Nation.*

in "The Snail," where the shell, obviously a room, becomes an inappropriate planet. The same kind of blurring characterizes his use of the color, yellow. Although he employs it thematically, as a sensory datum it is merely histrionic and, as a symbol, crudely approximate. It is advertising yellow. Indeed, the book is self-advertising. Consider the following sentimental poem (cited in its entirety):

> Chairs next to each other,
> I watch you, out of my tears,
> smiling at the corners of your mouth
> as the words reach me.

Self-pity and sentimentality don't wait long before biting back, and here's the very next poem (also in its entirety):

> You hate animals
> that kill birds.
> I see you under low leaves,
> eyes fixed.
> Claws extend in shadow.

In one poem only, the Rexrothian "Wood Smoke," Mr. Hall rises above mere talent, and almost combines skill and passion.

FROM THE SECOND GODINE POETRY, CHAPBOOK SERIES

☙ Roger Dickinson-Brown ❧

The Town of Hill, 1975

Donald Hall's *The Town of Hill* is terrible. Whatever talent
or promise there was in Hall's early books has almost entirely
given way to a formulaic pandering to the basest kind of popular
taste: I quote the whole of what I suppose is meant to be a zany
and charming poem:

FÊTE

      Festival lights go on
in villages throughout
      the province, from Toe
Harbor, past the
      Elbow Lakes, to Eyelid Hill
when you touch me, there.

Probably the most merciful thing that can be said about this
book is that is amounts to almost nothing. What there is, undis-
tinguished in language and rhythm, offensive, glib, and vain.
"I Lost My Overcoat in Omaha" is a typical poem of the kind
that used to be called refreshing:

Reprinted from *Southern Review*, by permission of the author. Copyright
© 1978 Roger Dickinson-Brown.

> Shirt, trousers, and one
> pair of underpants
> take breakfast and lunch
> on the nineteenth floor
> of the Fairmont, in San Francisco,
> directly over a red waterhole
> outside Milledgeville, Georgia.

The crowds at poetry readings who write and do not read poems must love it ("Poem With One Fact" contains the ironic or unironic line "If only we could *communicate* . . ."). "Professor Gratt" and "Eleanor's Letters" are at least a little offensive in their easy superiority to ordinary folks:

> He didn't *die*. That word
> Seemed harsh and arbitrary
> And thus was not preferred
> In her vocabulary.

But most of these poems are only rather silly and clumsy little crowd pleasers, written to dazzle the bourgeoisie, and too much has been said of them already.

ON *KICKING THE LEAVES*

⊂✗◦   Peter Stitt   ◦✗⊃

Kicking the Leaves, 1978

Kicking the Leaves by Donald Hall is an impressive volume, surely one of the best books of poetry published in 1978. It is also, in some ways, one of the strangest. Where does jacket copy come from anyway? Authors, do you write your own? Or do the publishers employ hacks, cast-out Hollywood agents perhaps, to perpetrate all these abuses? On this jacket we are told that, in the three years since Hall moved from Ann Arbor to New Hampshire, "the word has gone out: As he approaches fifty, back in the house where the poetry began, Hall has come into his own . . . This is a major book, the book that Hall's early admirers have been waiting and hoping for." Who sent the word out? And how? Did it come in on the AP wire while I was sleeping? Did Walter Cronkite say anything about it? Was it in *APR*? And what am I doing here? I thought it was my job, umpire on the diamond of poetry, to call the books and poems: Major! Minor! Disgusting! Should Never Have Been Published! Among the Masters! Should Have Been Published, But In Kuala Lumpur! Well, at least all those early admirers have permission to stop holding their breath.

The jacket singles out for praise three poems which, "in particular . . . brought Hall to the forefront of poetic attention" (what he is getting here is, alas, only prosaic attention)—"Kicking

Reprinted from *The Georgia Review*, by permission of the editor. Copyright © 1979 University of Georgia.

the Leaves," "Names of Horses," and "Eating the Pig." This brings up the second oddity about the book. It contains thirteen poems. The last nine deal brilliantly with the family farm in New Hampshire—where Hall spent summers as a boy, and to which he returned three years ago—with the family that lived there, with the pervasive subject of death. These poems form a tight unit and are obviously the substance and heart of the book. The other four poems, including "Eating the Pig," stand at the beginning; they both violate the spirit of the volume and constitute a parody of it. Briefly, if you want to parody a significant poet, all you need do is take the style and techniques which he applies to profound topics and apply them to trivial topics. This is what Hall has done to himself in these first four poems. I wish they weren't here; Hayden Carruth is certainly right in calling one of them, "O Cheese," the worst poem of the year.

But the other nine are easily among the best poems of the year. Because they are mostly quite long, it is hard to demonstrate fully their virtues. One of the strongest techniques used in the book is the reiteration within a given poem of a single image, which thus accrues meaning and can come to embody the emotional theme of the poem. "Flies" is a four-page prose poem; to quote all the passages where flies appear would be ludicrous— you would not be impressed. The theme is death, the passing and coming of generations—human and insectile. Hall describes the life and death of his grandmother, how on the farm she was always pestered by flies, how one buzzes as she dies. At the end of the poem, Hall awakens in her bedroom, himself of the third generation, and is bothered by a fly, "one of the hundred-thousandth generation." This synopsis is obviously flat; the poem is beautiful. Hall uses this technique over and over—with maple syrup, with black-faced sheep, with horses, with the leaves of the title poem.

And always he comes back to the subject of death—these poems are tender, affecting, loving elegies. "Name of Horses" delineates in general terms the life of a horse on the farm, from birth to death. As the poem concludes, Hall manages to compress history as he eulogizes several generations of horses:

> For a hundred and fifty years, in the pasture of dead horses,
>   roots of pine trees pushed through the pale curves of
>   your ribs,
> yellow blossoms flourished above you in autumn, and
>   in winter
> frost heaved your bones in the ground—old toilers,
>   soil makers:
>
> O Roger, Mackerel, Riley, Ned, Nellie, Chester, Lady Ghost.

A poem such as this, and they are nearly all like this, conveys a strong and elegiac sense of the past, of its relevance to and even presence within today.

The writing throughout this volume is first-rate; when Hall chooses to pull out all the stops and to show what he can do, the results are astonishing. "Stone Walls" begins:

> Stone walls emerge from leafy ground
> and show their bones. In September a leaf
> falls singly down, then a thousand leaves whirl
> in frosty air. I am wild
> with joy of leaves falling, of stone walls
> emerging, of return to the countryside
> where I lay as a boy
> in the valley of noon heat, in the village
> of little sounds; where I floated
> out of myself, into the world that lives in the air.

The passage takes its beauty from a careful use of assonance, chiefly in the *o* sounds, and consonance, chiefly in the *w*, *l*, *f*, and *s* sounds.

I confess that I do not have complete confidence in Donald Hall's judgment—primarily because of the first four poems here, but also because of the five short poems he recently published in *Poetry*. So I won't make any predictions for the future. But *Kicking the Leaves* is a magnificent book of poems; its power comes from Hall's uncanny way with words and from his reliance on a rich source of feeling—memories of his own past, legends of his family's past, myths attaching to the animals and the land. These are poems you will return to many times.

NEW HAMPSHIRE ELEGIES

Guy Davenport

Kicking the Leaves, 1978

Some poets eat; some do not. Homer ate (the plot of the *Odyssey* pivots on Odysseus' refusing deifying ambrosia nectar at the table of the jerkwater nymph Calypso, dismissing immortality for his Penelope's home cooking; hence Joyce's introduction of his plebeian Odysseus with: "Mr. Leopold Bloom ate with relish the inner organs of beasts and fowls"), but not so much as an antipasto gets passed around in all of Dante. Chaucer ate (chickens boiled in their marybones, topped off by a blackmanger, pop up quite soon in *The Canterbury Tales*); Walter Savage Landor ate (rhyming "venison" with "Tennyson"). Who can imagine an ode to a pot roast by Matthew Arnold?

Alkman sang the roasted chickpea; Sappho, celery; but where in Poe will you find a plate of grits and gravy? A theory lurks somewhere hereabouts: something to do with candor, feet on the ground, geniality.

The first of Donald Hall's poems in his new collection is a meditation on roast pig; the second celebrates cheeses; the third is about eating a wolf; the fourth begins, "After the many courses, hot bowls of rice, / plates of pork, cabbage, ducks, and peapods . . . ." The fifth is titled "Maple Syrup."

And yet all the poems in *Kicking the Leaves* are about death, not food. Their persistent elegiac tone rises first of all from that roast pig, who — apple in mouth — in its anatomical wholeness touches the poet's sense of pity and starts him thinking about ancient modes of cooking when stoves were altars, slaughter was sacrifice, and ceremony attended both the death and the ingestion of animals. In primitive cultures there is a pact between hunter and hunted, sealed with an oath. Artemis, goddess of the hunt, was also the goddess of mercy. Eating in its archaic moment was religion (magic, if you will). To eat tiger was to appropriate ferociousness.

As with Odysseus, food means home. The real cradle of our souls is the family table. If Heaven intends to reward me with bliss, it will have to serve me blackberry cobbler, nickel shrimp sauteed in butter, country ham, and buttermilk. Food takes Donald Hall's heart back to his family's rhythms of seasons and deaths, back to his memories of his great-grandfather's farm in New Hampshire which is now his own.

So rich a theme has generated poems about roses, horses, oxcarts, black-faced sheep. Hall writes with clarity and honesty, enlisting none of the usual strategies of poetry such as rhyme, meter, or a heightened diction. His words are plain and right, and his manner is casual and alert. At the center of the book is a poem about kicking leaves while walking home from a football game with his wife and children — a meditative, childish, idle thing to do. He stirs memories along with the leaves: the autumnal tone of the day deepens the elegiac music of his lines. He treads leaves, knee-deep in death, and foresees his own death with a kind of acceptance, "the pleasure, the only long pleasure, of taking a place in the story of leaves."

These poems are a celebration, as he makes clear, of the poet's middle age. They are a stock-taking, a sifting of values. The raw and unsettling evocations of death by violence (of wolves, pigs, people) are, it would seem, deliberate encounters with reality to be faced with a naked mind, wihtout religion or philosophy. And, it must be added, without sentimentality or romantic coloring.

The taste these poems leave in the mind is the bitterness of life's brevity, the disgust we hide from ourselves at having to slaughter to live. Against the goodness of being alive runs the harshness of the bargains by which we live: the toil and death of other creatures both animal and human. This is a bleak way of looking at things. It is, in part, the way these poems look at the world. Such honesty has its reward. There are lights other than the worst to see things in, and, having insisted on the shadows, Hall feels free to exult in brightnesses.

Pity is an ambiguous emotion , part fear and part solicitude. Hall has purged fear from his pity (a purging that may be the theme that brings these poems into a unity), giving a kind of awe to his solicitude for the fragility and uncertainty of life.

One of the most moving poems in this book is an elegy to old farm horses whose lives are ended with a shotgun. The last line is a masterly roll of their names: "O Roger, Mackerel, Riley, Ned, Nellie, Chester, Lady Ghost."

HANDING OVER THE PAST

Richard Jackson

Kicking the Leaves, 1978

In "Stone Walls," the final poem in Donald Hall's *Kicking the Leaves*, the poet, remembering his grandfather, tells how "riding home from the hayfields, he handed me the past." It is just such a "handing over" that Hall extends in this flawless and moving book. That past, as he suggests later in "Stone Walls," is a complex arrangement of perspectives, social, personal and geological: Allende, the Shah of Iran, Tiberius, a slain grocer; his own family history; the "jamming plates" of the Appalachian range which formed the White Mountains of New Hampshire where he now lives, and the retreat of glaciers even as there were "Siberian eyes / tracking bear ten thousand years ago / on Kearsage."

The basis of this handing over of the past is what Hall calls a "return" to the very origins of the conscious self:

> I am wild
> with the joy of leaves falling, of stone walls
> emerging, of return to the countryside
> where I lay as a boy
> in the valley of noon heat, in the village
> of little sounds; where I floated
> out of myself, into the world that lives in the air.

The counterpointing of past and present which constitutes the "return" provides the basis for a system of balances that is

Reprinted from *Prairie Schooner*, by permission of University of Nebraska Press. Copyright © 1979 University of Nebraska Press.

gradually modulated — between floating and falling; by the movement into the past self, then out of that self, then into past
imaginings; between these dynamics of motion and the stasis
of the reclining boy; between that solitary boy in the countryside
and his "village / of little sounds," and so on.

These balances are sustained, here and throughout the book,
by the repetition and variation of vowel sounds, the easy con-
traction and expansion of line lengths (one remembers Hall's
definition of "form" in the conclusion to his recent *Remembering
Poets*: "minute resolutions of vowel and metaphor, consonant
and idea, by which the poem finds its requisite wholeness").
These balances inherent in the "return" also suggest a pattern
of compensations — the very barrenness of autumn allows the
old stone walls to be seen, and the stone walls themselves,
"emerging" each autumn, are man's counterpart to the
"unperishing hills," to the cyclic nature of the seasons. The impulse to "return" to the "world that lives in the air," then, is
not finally a metaphysical or transcendental one; the aim and
the difficulty Hall confronts in this book are to "float out of
the self" and yet "walk on the earth of the present."

The way to the "return" is opened up by a realization of how
all things, on a very physical level, interpenetrate. In "Maple
Syrup" a quart of syrup made twenty-five years ago by Hall's
now dead grandfather, and now recently discovered, serves as
a vehicle for this physical transcendence:

> taste
> the sweetness, you for the first time,
> the sweetness preserved, of a dead man
> in his own kitchen,
> giving us
> from his lost grave the gift of sweetness.

In a sense the "return" (note here the returns of "sweetness") as an *emergence* of new relations, is always a beginning, a "first time," an enterprise for the future. So the character in "Ox Cart Man" each year sells all his farm products, including his cart, and then returns home to spend the winter making a new cart for the next year. So, Hall says in "Flies," returning to an old saying as he remembers his grandparents' deaths, and imagining himself filling their place: "The blow of the axe resides in the acorn."

Precisely what Donald Hall establishes by his "returns," his sense of "emergence" of the past and self, precisely how he hands himself over, are the underlying concerns of the whole volume. The title poem, which like "Stone Walls" is in several impressionistically connected parts, uses the repeated activity of kicking up autumn leaves to link several time periods and to provide a symbolic action linking the parts of the poem: "Kicking up the leaves, I uncover the lids of graves." It is an activity that not only recalls the deaths of his father and grand-father, but seems, in retrospect, to have foreshadowed them; kicking the leaves in Ann Arbor years later, Hall remembers "kicking the leaves, / autumn 1955 in Massachusetts knowing / my father would die when the leaves were gone." In a similar way, watching his own son and daughter grow old and distance themselves as they create their own lives, he projects: "I / diminish, not them; as I go first / into the leaves, taking / the steps they will follow, Octobers and years from now." What allows such an imaginative step is the fact that

> This year the poems came back, when the leaves fell.
> Kicking the leaves, I heard the leaves tell stories,
> remembering, and therefore looking ahead, and building
> the house of dying. I looked up into the maples
> and found them, the vowels of bright desire.

Hall's is a poetics, not only in this poem but throughout the
book, predicated on death, on a return to and emergence from
past deaths, on a joyful handing over of the self defined by his
own future death. It is a poetics where, to paraphrase a thesis
from *Remembering Poets*, the life in him is too strong for the
death in him:

> Now I leap and fall, exultant, recovering
> from death, on account of death, in accord with the dead,
> the smell and taste of leaves again,
> and the pleasure, the only long pleasure, of taking a place
> in the story of leaves.

FROM A BABEL OF TONGUES

Vernon Shetley ౭ఴ

Kicking the Leaves, 1978

Donald Hall's *Kicking the Leaves* shows Hall working within one of the more prevalent styles of the day; lacking a better term, one might call it neo-Georgian. Outwardly, this mode derives from William Carlos Williams; it observes the limits of common speech, uses a relaxed free verse, and exalts the commonplace, trusting that the ideas in things are ideas enough. The paradise it loses and regains is usually that of Midwestern life, not today's suburbia and agribusiness, but the innocent small town-rural world of the depression or war era. Indeed Hall departs from Williams most significantly in just this regard; as opposed to the rich sense of the immediate one finds in Williams, Hall continually recedes from the present into a remembered childhood.

This is not in itself a bad thing, and some of Hall's best effects come from a shuttling or suspension between two times and thus two states of mind. But the poems frequently show an excessive particularity that makes them into individual nostalgias: not grammar school, but Spring Glen grammar school, not church, but South Danbury Church. Hall seems intent on possessing, alone, the realm of his poetry rather than letting the reader enter it as an emblematic world. One feels at times as if one had intruded on a family reunion. Directly

Reprinted from *Poetry*, by permission of the editor. Copyright © 1979 The Modern Poetry Association.

in the pastoral tradition, these poems aim, by recovering the
time of the poet's innocence, to recover the time of the world's
innocence. Yet the poems fall ultimately short of revivifying
their conventions; they too often fall prey to a kind of rural
picturesqueness:

> and riding home from the hayfields, he handed me
> > the past
> how he walked on a row of fenceposts
> in the blizard of eighty-eight; or sawed oblongs
> of ice from Eagle Pond; or in summer
> drove the hayrack into shallow water, swelling wooden
> wheels tight inside iron rims;
> or chatted and teased outside Amos Johnson's with
> > Buffalo Billy
> Fiske who dressed like a cowboy . . .

True though they may be, such details evoke not rural life but
a popular sentimentalization of it; Hall succumbs to the Angelic
parody of his genre. Hall aspires to an unmediated sincerity and
intimacy with the reader, but his method is, paradoxically,
academic. He applies a series of formulas to theme and language,
and in so doing, seems to alienate himself from his experience.

FROM SHORT REVIEWS

❧ David Shapiro ☙

The Happy Man, 1986

Donald Hall's eighth book of poems is a very powerful volume, and it makes a rare combination of phantasmal and shattering narratives with natural description of high precision. His descriptions of cows, chickens, and some convincingly Chaucerian fowl are massed with the colorful modulation that make them more than impressionist. There is a reflexive joy in Hall's language that does not hinder an equal and impassioned joy in mimesis itself. Another poet I admire is conjured in these poems, James Schuyler, and the landscape here has a patient particularism and a grace analogous to Schuyler's but with an idiosyncratic melancholy that is quite identifiably Hall's: "It is good / to wake early in high / summer with work to do, / and look out the window / at a ghost bird lifting away / to drowse all morning / in his grassy hut" ("Whip-poor-will"). Since Hall is capable of a dense prose and can use this prosiness well within his poetry, one has to admire the winnowing here, the modest "clear brief notes" of a poem terse in its custom-made crispness, the summery laconism of the lyric lament that reads as paradoxical praise. It is not for nothing that this highly polarized volume, oscillating between calm representation and agitated introspection, quotes the mystic Eckhart on the power of Repose. Haunted by a father's dying face, the poet turns to "building a house" as a central sacred act in a world more profaned than the word. Building a landscape, building up a dream sequence, and constructing a sufficient dwelling are the soul-making tasks here.

Again and again, Hall shows his resonant power in constructing voices, as it were, voices placed in such a way as to give us a kind of rural antidote to the conventional urban Waste Land. It is a note-worthy and adequately multiple pastorale, and it is of course elegiac. The son recalls the exasperated father and his longings to do only what one desires. The enormously moving fragment, "Shrubs Burnt Away," from a long poem in progress, keeps up a steady and ambiguous marriage of voices, childhood reminiscences, and a final mating on a joyful central bed. The image that an archetypal psychologist might hunt for most diligently is laid bare immediately: a secret house constructed by a brother and sister out of some precise Märchen. But we are not permitted mere enchantment for long, as the poet gives us a father weeping in rage over the cradle, and the ravelled children grow amidst adulteries and wars into the possible consolations of a craftman's middle age. This long poem has a power of a novella, full of a strong *black-white* in the Japanese sense. One does not forget that, in the Chinese tradition, Tu Fu's central poem is that of his house blown to pieces by the autumn wind, where the poet dreams in an emergency of the poor scholars of the whole world and a house that could contain them like a mountain. Hall contributes to our most dignified sense, with his recollections of failure and interruptions of rapport, of a public dream of shared and secret space.

The poet has come upon a plain style that is still sensual, filled with parallelism and play, capable of solemnity and a flexible humor. The image of an inexhaustible joy contrasts with the Virgilian twilight that always touched his mind:

From the Studebaker's backseat, on our Sunday drives,
I watched her earrings sway. Then I walked uphill
beside an old man carrying buckets
under birches on an August day. Striding at noontime,
I looked at wheat and at river cities. In the crib
my daughter sighed opening her eyes. I kissed the cheek
of my father dying. By the pond an acorn fell.
You listening here, you reading these words as I write them,
I offer this cup to you: Though we drink
from this cup every day, we will never drink it dry.

(from *The Day I Was Older*)

This marvelous elegy to the world without marvels is the final proportionate gift of the "happy man" of the ironic and truthful title. The guilty innocent son has outlived the imperfect, loved, entangling father. The poet reads the obituaries and is a professional reader, *at the sign of the signs*. The world has become as reposeful as the patrician landscapes of a Fairfield Porter, whose chief message, he remarked to this critic once, was: "Conclude every sermon with the words, Pay attention." The poet pays attention to each part of the kingdom: "A mink scuds through ferns; an acorn tumbles." It is a kind of ode to "To Autumn," an homage to unexplained and inexplicable particulars. But the poet cannot end without noting that the family is part of landscape and makes for the bread and wine of miraculous largesse. What Hall achieves here and elsewhere is a kind of psalm to the passage, as Freud put it, from hysterical misery to ordinary unhappiness. But ordinary unhappiness is our most appropriate form of happiness. This is a poetics of imperfection, one that regards all Utopian notions of purity as what Meyer Schapiro called a hypothesis. The imperfect reader, not Joyce's ideal reader with ideal insomnia, is offered the resource of the poet's desire for clear representation.

Buckminster Fuller once suggested a gigantic bubble over the metropolis of modernity to accomplish, among other things, the end of deleterious weather. Donald Hall, like Fairfield Porter, laughs at such a sad unwillingness to accept contingency, and his most sensual poems concern the wild irregular regularities of inner and outer weather. (The reader of his rich, almost Elizabethan "Twelve Seasons," might also want to look up Hall's prose homage to winter in the haunting catalogue for a show of paintings called *Winter,* published last year by the Hood Museum of Art.) Hall's love for particularity in nature would have cheered the empiricist in Fairfield Porter, who recounted to me his delight in watching the Fuller domes get tossed by the Maine breeze. Fuller was involved in the distribution of clear information, while art revels in "disastrous relationships." Hall is particularly thrilling on the happy disasters of relations, and the relative happiness of a starry fall.

THE POET AS A PERFECTIONIST

Tom Clark

The Happy Man, 1986

Donald Hall's eminence as an editor, teacher and critic of verse has had the ironic effect of overshadowing his own poems, an effect enhanced in recent years by his reticence about publishing new work.

Hall is an extreme example of the perfectionist poet, one who writes his poems over and over again until sometimes the copious re-draftings add up to as many pages as the manuscript of a novel. In his pursuit of a poetry worthy of eternity, he refuses to settle for near misses. *The Happy Man* (the first collection of his to appear in eight years) lives up to Hall's own high standard. His eighth collection of poems in 31 years, it marks a major advance for him, particularly in its strategic use of dramatic voices.

The longest and most difficult piece here, "Shrubs Burnt Away" (one section, he informs us in a note, of an even longer work), takes Hall's new dramatic method to its extreme, with a multivoiced, elliptical narrative that has the disjointed structure of a disturbing dream. The most arresting of its voices is that of a lonely, troubled, middle-aged man who numbs himself with whiskey every evening, in his home or out in the faceless neon American motel night.

This troubled man's voice is a kind of ground bass in *The*

Happy Man, making its title deeply ironic. If the man in "Shrubs Burnt Away" tells himself, six scotches down the line, that he's "very happy," it's clearly a precarious happiness, the thin ice over waters of breakup and breakdown whose chill is almost tangible.

That voice comes back in two impressive dramatic monologues at the center of the book, "My Friend Felix" and "Merle Bascom's .22." The former's middle-aged narrator, driving across Texas, is joined by the apparition of an old friend who has been dead 30 years—"my lucky friend Felix." A sudden brush with automotive death coaxes a revelatory message out of this ghost. The brush with highway death recurs in "Merle Bascom's .22," where the association of sudden death with revelation is even closer.

Conflicting senses of mortality are currents that govern this book. Alternately, Hall proposes the sweet temptation of death as ultimate release and the dread and grief of death as terminal closure; they are emotional pulls that wisely he allows to remain in tension, unresolved and unreconciled in these poems as they are in life.

The New Hampshire farm poems early in *The Happy Man* show Hall's pastoral understanding; in the later poems the pastoral image is threatened by other, darker images that close in by stages, like wolves encircling a pasture at twilight. The poems show a love of the sun, the upward process of growth and the green fields of daylight—but also a strong sense of a very different kind of natural force, which pulls at us from the other direction.

This downward pull is embodied with reductive eloquence in the dramatic figuration of the book's finest pieces—like the small lament for ex-baseball hero Ted Williams on Old Timers'

Day in "Couplet," where Williams, lumbering to catch a fly ball, becomes a fallen god, a divine warrior brought low by time's gravity on the bright playing surface / battlefield. "We rise," Hall writes,

> and applaud weeping:
> On a green field
> we observe the ruin
> of even the bravest
> body as Odysseus
> wept to glimpse
> among the shades the shadow
> of Achilles.

The craftsmanship for which Donald Hall has often been praised is responsible for maneuvering the syntax of those lines so adroitly, but the elegiac power there is something new for this fine poet.

HYMNING THE HUMDRUM

Dean Wilson

The Happy Man, 1986

In *The Happy Man*, his eighth collection of verse, Donald Hall discovers a range and intensity of voice one could hardly have guessed at from most of his earlier work. Hall is one of the most professional and committed of American poets, and it is exciting to find dedication to his craft being so richly rewarded.

Hall grew up on a small farm in Connecticut, and has written many poems celebrating the simplicities of small-town America. *The Happy Man* opens with a batch of these that are frankly nostalgic, though not idyllic. A little like Frost in this respect, he seems to take a special delight in images of the super-annuated: old men crouched over winter fires, a dairy-farmer found dead at his milk-pail, leaning "into the side of his last Holstein," the last dance of a beheaded rooster before he's plucked and boiled for a Sunday fricassee.

These are short stories developed swiftly and unsentimen-tally, but in the longest poem in the book, "Shrubs Burnt Away," Hall tries his hand at a full-length poetic narrative (whether he succeeds or not is hard to tell, as this is only the first section of a projected book-length poem, to be called *Build a House*). His method here is more complex, but basically there are two main stories — each with various subplots — interleaved together seemingly at random. In one a young woman artist is pursued by nightmares of grotesque physical dismemberment inherited from an alcoholic mother; in the other a character who might be out of Martin Amis's fiction leaves his wife and children for life on the booze in the motels of Hollywood. Hall is aiming here, as the title suggests, at the bleakest, least encumbered view of life he can imagine, but the austerity isn't exactly Beckettian:

> Studying a bikini'd
> photograph on a matchbook, I dial BONNIE FASHION
> MODEL AVAILABLE at four in the morning
> from my vinyl room, and the answering service tells me
> that Bonnie is out to lunch....

More unambiguously successful are the last two sections of the book, "Men Driving Cars" and "Sisters," and the male and female contrasts they develop. In these, Hall is especially good at exploiting ordinariness, at making the humdrum somehow satisfying. These poems are so unspectacular they seem almost expected, the sort of poems about the sort of things—a baseball match, acorns, even one on Keats and Fanny Brawne—that practically anyone could write if they put their minds to it.

This obviousness, though, is probably Hall's greatest strength. Like Hardy's, his poetry often seems most relaxed and interesting when it sounds most like a high-school exercise. His has always been a malleable talent, but not all his experiments have come off. He suffered especially in the late 1960s when forms loosened up, and he plunged into a wild surrealistic phase ("Buick of yellow leaves, sing the peanut wheel!") full of second-hand Ginsberg and O'Hara. In The Happy Man his voice emerges as distinctly his own in a language unemphatic and flexible enough to deal with the commonest experience.

ON *THE HAPPY MAN*

Peter Stitt

The Happy Man, 1986

In *The Happy Man*, his eighth book of poetry, Donald Hall's best poems nestle significant images within an overall narrative flow. And while there are some excellent shorter pieces here that employ imagery with only the slightest trace of narrative, there are none that reverse this pattern of imbalance. Though the passage of time in "Whip-poor-will" is very short, it is enough to give a narrative basis to an otherwise imagistic poem:

> As the last light
> of June withdraws
> the whip-poor-will sings
> his clear brief notes
> by the darkening house, then
> rises abruptly from sandy
> ground, a brown bird
> in the near-night, soaring
> over shed and woodshed
> to far dark fields. When
> he returns at dawn,
> in my sleep I hear
> his three syllables make
> a man's name, who slept
> fifty years in this bed
> and ploughed these fields:

> *Wes-ley-Wells . . . Wes-*
> *ley-Wells . . .* It is good
> to wake early in high
> summer with work to do,
> and look out the window at a ghost bird lifting away
> to drowse all morning
> in his grassy hut.

Donald Hall is well known for several characteristic concerns, each of which appears in this poem. There is his almost Frostian celebration of nature and the land, his profound sense of the past (both personal and communal), his love of hard work in early morning, and his understanding of the persistence of elegy. All of these are introduced through a single carefully developed image, the bird and the bird's song.

Although this is not apparent from the poem just discussed, *The Happy Man* does not come by its title easily. That the volume is preoccupied with the passage of time and the progress of death we see most clearly in the long narrative poems that form the bulk of its substance. Dominant among them is the unified central part, "Shrubs Burnt Away," which the poet describes as one section of a three-part poem still under composition. It portrays a character with no settled sense of direction, definitely not a happy man. The poem seems fragmentary as it shifts quickly and frequently from time to time and place to place—though its sections are held together by certain repeated and developed images, most notably what Hall calls "the house of dying" and the white hairs the speaker finds growing on his wrist. Interspersed with this man's story is that of a woman, similarly lost, whom we see grow ever more neurotic with each word she speaks—much like the woman whose letters are quoted in Williams Carlos Williams' *Paterson*. It is easy to

guess that Hall has positioned this fragment at the center of
his book to highlight the settled maturity of the speaking voice
in the rest of the poems. The piece is so unusual within Hall's
oeuvre that one waits with considerable interest to see how it
will be finished.

More typical of Hall's imagistic narrative method is "The Day
I Was Older," which concludes the volume. Each of the poem's
five, ten-line stanzas is given a subtitle to indicate its central
image or idea. The first of these, "The Clock," begins with a
comparison the poet will find useful: "The clock on the parlor
wall, stout as a mariner's clock, / disperses the day." All night
long it tolls the half-hour and the hour as "Warm / in the dark
next to your breathing, / below the thousand favored stars, I
feel / horns of gray water heave / underneath us, and the ship's
pistons / pound as the voyage continues over the limited sea."
The simple image of the clock is opened out, through metaphor,
into a vision of the passing of life's time.

This slight intimation of mortality is extended and localized
in the next stanza, "The News," where the speaker describes
his obsessive reading of the obituaries in the morning paper.
He discovers that a former lover, Emily Farr, has died: "Once
in an old house we talked for an hour, while a coalfire / brightened in November twilight and wavered / our shadows high
on the wall / until our eyes fixed on each other. Thirty years
ago." The linkage of death with beloved woman is carried one
step further in the third stanza, "The Pond," where the speaker
suffers a frightening vision while admiring his current love: "You
do not know that I am watching, taking pleasure / in your
breasts that rise and fall as you breathe. / Then I see mourners
gathered by an open grave."

"The Day" of the title ("The Day I Was Older") is described

in the poem's penultimate stanza: "Last night at suppertime I outlived my father, enduring / the year, month, day, and hour / when he lay back on a hospital bed in the guestroom / among cylinders of oxygen—mouth open, nostrils and lips / fixed un-quivering, pale blue." In these lines the speaker feels the lesson of mortality so personally that we can almost hear him gasp. The poem has reached a culmination of sorts; up to this point, Hall has presented a powerful series of events, feelings, and images, all of them conspiring to make the speaker feel lonely, vulnerable, mortal, and old. In the concluding stanza, entitled "The Cup," he changes his strategy in an interesting way:

> From the Studebaker's backseat, on our Sunday drives,
> I watched her earrings sway. Then I walked uphill
> beside an old man carrying buckets
> under birches on an August day. Striding at noontime,
> I looked at wheat and at river cities. In the crib
> my daughter sighed opening her eyes. I kissed the cheek
> of my father dying. By the pond an acorn fell.
> You listening here, you reading these words as I write them,
> I offer this cup to you: Though we drink
> from this cup every day, we will never drink it dry.

Like the entire book, this poem does not tell a single story that flows, in a straight line, from beginning to end. Each of the earlier stanzas describes, almost in circular fashion, a single event or image selected from a limited period of time in the speaker's life. We move forward in fits and starts. Then, in the first eight lines of the final stanza, we see a truncated version of this method; Hall presents a quick series of seven treasured memories, some of them events (kissing his dying father) and some of them images (earrings, acorn). The final lines of the stanza, which also conclude the book, provide a generalized, imagistic explana-tion of why these are the poems of a happy man. Again like the entire book, it is an impressive and moving performance. Always a writer of great intellectual power, Donald Hall has consolidated, in *The Happy Man*, the increased emotional depth evident in his work since *Kicking the Leaves* (1978).

THE HAPPY MAN

David St. John

The Happy Man, 1986

In *String Too Short to Be Saved*, his marvelous book of recollections of his childhood summers at Eagle Pond Farm, Donald Hall recounts memories and narratives of a time and place he thought was forever lost to him. Yet because the world is a mysterious and sometimes generous place, Hall found himself living at Eagle Pond Farm (where his great-grandfather had begun farming in 1865) in the fall of 1975, and he has lived there ever since. Hall's remarkable collection of poems, *Kicking the Leaves* (1978) was the announcement and celebration of that homecoming, that return to New Hampshire.

String Too Short to Be Saved is a loving album of family portraits, landscape sketches, and quiet paeans to the rural values Hall recalled. *Kicking the Leaves* became Hall's farewell to his life in Ann Arbor ("a life of parties and schools, lectures and plays, English departments and picnics, tennis, tenure and Volvos"), as he stepped simultaneously back into his past and forward into his future, into the hope that any new life carries with it.

Kicking the Leaves is a compelling and powerful volume of poems. Deceptively straightforward in its style, the book is haunting in its human resonances. It is a book in which a man makes peace with the natural world — with the land, in this case

First appeared in *Western Humanities Review*, Vol. XLI, No. 4 (Winter 1987). Copyright © 1987 David St. John.

the rugged and beautiful landscape of southern New Hampshire, and with its animals, seen by Hall with a sense of loving kinship.

In his return, Hall found his own place in a lineage of values, his own rightful inheritance in a world of *trust*, and work; he found *his* place in a real place, a physical landscape — not in a place of the imagination, of the mind. And not, I should add, in an unlived landscape, but a landscape with a history that was both personal and familial.

In the poems of *Kicking the Leaves*, we see how Eagle Pond Farm becomes both a source and a resource for Hall. Even the harshness and elemental quality of rural farm life give, with the dailiness of physical work, a kind of clarifying urgency. The poems all become hymns of praise for the men and women and animals that populate, or once populated, the farm and its surrounding villages. For Hall, the farm quietly came to represent the timelessness of place, a timelessness he could see reflected in the mountains around him. In the face of the shifting horrors of contemporary life and politics, this created, for the speaker of these poems, a place of solace, a vantage point of strong witness. And at the end of the book *Kicking the Leaves*, in the poem "Stone Walls," Donald Hall is exactly where he wishes to be:

> Pole beans raise their green flags in the summer garden.
> I grow old, in the house I wanted to grow old in.
> When I am sleepy at night, I daydream only
> of waking the next morning—to walk on the earth of
>   the present
> past noons of birch and sugarbush, past cellarholes,
> many miles to the village of nightfall.

Yet in his new collection, *The Happy Man*, Hall can see in the distance that "the village of nightfall" is all too quickly approaching.

* * *

In *The Happy Man*, Donald Hall may indeed still be as happy as ever, yet the sunlit vistas of the past are now shown complete with their complicated shadows. One has only to note the book's marvelous and scary epigraph from Tolstoy for the title to acquire its proper irony:

> Behold me then, a man happy and in good health, hiding the rope in order not to hang myself to the rafters of the room where every night I went to sleep alone; behold me no longer shooting, lest I should yeild to the too easy temptation. . .

Hall introduces his new volume with a section of ghosts, both animal and human; he is a conjurer who summons, in "Great Day in the Cows' House," the spirit of his grandfather and those of his grandfather's cows! The effect is startling and poignant; we feel ourselves drawn slowly into the living pulse of the natural world, yet of the natural world that belonged to Hall's dead grandfather. Of these spirits, we presume, of those that follow in this opening section, Hall says, "They are long dead; they survive. . . ."

The presence of this past, its men and women and landscapes, invades every poem in *The Happy Man*, but it's nowhere more explicitly apparitional than in this opening section. In "Whippoor-will" the poet is summoned to the day by a "ghost bird" calling him by a ghostly name—the name of his dead grandfather, whose place he has taken. "Scenic View" provides its ghost mountains, a landscape certain to take its vengeance upon the tourists who've drained it of color with their endless photography. "The Rocker" supports a grandmother and her story, a ghost story of a suicide. The poem concludes: "Her kettle

steams; / her fat old tomcat / turns his head / when a mouse
skitters / over linoleum." The unrelentingly predatory quality
of nature and natural processes, of which time's ravagement is
one, is present everywhere in *The Happy Man*. Here is one of
the stanzas of the poem "Twelve Seasons":

> A doe walks in the railroad's trench on corrupt snow.
> Her small hooves poke holes in the crust,
> melted and frozen again, that scrapes her ankles
> as her starved head swivels for bark. So the dogpack,
> loosened one by one from stove-warm houses, gathers
> seven leaping bodies that larrup, sliding
> along the crust, like twelve-year-old boys at recess
> chasing a sissy. They rip her throat out.
> Walking on a mild day, as snow melts from the tracks,
> we find the body hollowed by birds and coyotes
> and drag it aside, into a grove of yellow birch
> that beavers forested, leaving spiky stumps behind.

In "Twelve Seasons" (a poem of twelve stanzas of twelve lines
each), Hall recounts a passage through real seasons and seasons
of memory. The poem is a meditation on aging and survival,
strength and fortitude, the brother-and-sisterhood of the old
and the young. Hall says, "Ghosts rise, ghosts whirl in the afternoon leaves, / as the dead visit the declining year. We take them
in. . . ." Indeed, there is a place for the dead in this cycle of
seasons. Hall treasures these passages and the human resilience
they reveal. The poem concludes in this lovely and ambigous
way; it is winter, December:

> Now we gather in the black evening, in Advent,
> as our nervous and reasonable fingers continually reach
> for the intangible. Now we wait together;
> we add wood to the castiron stove, and midnight's

> candlelight trembles on the ceiling
> as we drowse waiting. Someone is at the door.

The second section of *The Happy Man* is the single long poem "Shrubs Burnt Away" (which is one part of a projected book-length poem to be entitled *Build A House*), a startling and riveting meditation on mortality and aspects of self-destruction. The poem takes its title from this passage from Hsu Hsia-K'o: "Mi-t'o Temple after thirty li. A most desolate spot . . . For fear of hiding tigers, all trees and shrubs have been burnt." As "Shrubs Burnt Away" progresses, we increasingly recognize the irony of this passage (an epigraph to the poem), as we see that the most serious predators of the lives recounted—madness and alcoholism and adultery—arise from within those lives. And, sadly, we see the elements of self-destruction as that paradoxical burning away of the shrubs.

The project of this ambitious poem is to build a house of the spirit, and to build it from within the house of the body, by definition already a corrupted house, a house which will fall—a house of death. "Shrubs Burnt Away" opens with a mother's tale to a sleepy child, a tale of a brother and sister who build a secret house in the woods. This ideal of refuge then gives way immediately to the poem's next scene in which the poet, middle-aged, "starting / the night's bottle," says, "I daydream to build / the house of dying. . . ."

Flights—both flights from difficulty and real flights in the early history of air navigation—weave their metaphorical escapes throughout the poem, as the corruptions of place (Hollywood and Sunset Strip) begin to mirror the self-inflicted corruptions of the body, alcoholism and destructive cigarette smoking (from which the poet's father, we learn, has died). And the "real"

flights, we should note, are all flights of unfortunate consequences, from Wrong-Way Corrigan to Amelia Earhart.

The only proper adjective for this poem is *searing*. There is
such an extraordinarily complex investigation of the psyche at
work here; using filmic shifts of time and locale, Hall is able
to trace the threads of disintegration through the lives of his
speakers (there are two speakers here, a man and a woman) and
his incidental characters as well. Hall, in this poem, wants to
confront the violence one finds not only in the external world,
but also within himself—or herself, as the case may be—as well.
Again, the insistence of mortality drives every line.

"Shrubs Burnt Away" reveals all of the tigers still lurking in
our lives. The house of marriage collapses; the poet says, "I told
my wife: Consider me a wind / that lifts square houses up and
spins them / into each other. . . ." The male speaker in the poem
is often adrift, numbed; he is a false Sinbad, an adventurer who
can't make it off the motel-room bed. The house of sexuality
seems to tremble everywhere around him, but the true home
of the sensual, nowhere. The poem concludes with the male
speaker, "waking dozing twisted in the damp clothes / of lethargy,
loathing, and the desire to die." The female speaker, in her last
address, recounts a vision in which "the children," who one
presumes are her own, are sentenced to death; a "visitor" then
enters her kitchen to give her a lesson, using a rag-doll and
scissors, in how to then dismember them—"as I must do," the
speaker says, "as it seems that I want to do."

The horrors of "Shrubs Burnt Away" are all the more stunning as the reader comes to understand how much they are
all horrors of consciousness and self-consciousness. Can art,
can poetry do anything to mitigate the force of these horrors?

The stringent conscience that arises from the objectified diction of "Shrubs Burnt Away" has two functions: the first, to imply yes, art can; and the second, to keep the poem from crumbling under the force of its emotions. The poem has a second epigraph, central to this question, which forces us to recognize that much of the project of this poem has been to make poetry out of what cannot become poetry. It also leads us to question the premise from which the poem sets out. From Matthew Arnold: "What then are the situations, from the representation of which, though accurate, no poetical enjoyment can be derived? They are those in which the suffering finds no vent in action; in which a continuous state of mental distress is prolonged, unrelieved by incident, hope, or resistance; in which there is everything to be endured, nothing to be done." It is from precisely this state that this spectacular poem emerges.

Hall conjures, in the third section of *The Happy Man*, voices and characters both local and historical, from his acquaintances, literature, and even baseball. The baseball poems are always, of course, more about the passing of time than the crack of the bat (though perhaps those two are the same). Here, in every poem, we find lives emptied out by circumstance, by time. These are in some ways the voices of living ghosts, women and men who've suffered great losses, whose voices rest at the edge of violence, each in danger of imploding. These are characters latent with anger and frustration, figures doing their best to simply keep on. For me, the most frightening aspect of several of these poems is their composure in the face of great internal pressure, in the face of the fragmentation of a life. The characters are, one feels, each, in his or her own choice of life over death, spectacularly courageous. The "affliction" of the soul each faces becomes the occasion for Hall's meditations, several in the form of monologues. Again, our undeniable transience on earth and the "concealment" of life's terrors beneath its glossy surface are the facts that trouble each of these poems. Yet these are all speakers who tell themselves the truth; they confront, despair, and prevail. Even their own self-loathing engenders in us, because of the lack of self-pity, only the most generous response. In this section, entitled "Men Driving Cars," the men of these poems all believed they were going *somewhere*, only to find they had no destination at all.

What, then, does the soul look toward in this fragmented world? Hall provides a partial answer in his epigraph to the concluding section of the book, a passage from Meister Eckhart (a presiding spirit in *The Happy Man*): "If I were asked to tell the truth about God's purposes, when he created us, I would say 'Repose.' If I were asked what the soul looked for I would answer: 'Repose.' If I were asked what all creatures wanted, in all their natural efforts and motions, I would answer: 'Repose.'" This section, entitled "Sisters," once again makes peace with the world, the natural world. The women in these poems become "sisters" in spirit to the men driving cars. The poems urge us towards a sense of kinship, of brother-and-sisterhood with the natural world, its people and animals, its grasses, its stones. We are, after all, the most transitory aspect of this planet of grass and earth; yet it is essential, Hall repeatedly shows, that we not forget that we are *of* this world. In the poem "Granite and Grass," Hall notes that we worship granite as an "emblem of permanence," yet it is only the grass which "generates again" each spring. Nature's cycles of recomposition and regeneration mirror the mortal, yet the changing is, therefore, everlasting. The last stanza of this poem reads:

> Ragged Mountain was granite before Adam divided.
> Grass lives because it dies. If weary of discord

we gaze heavenward through the same eye that looks at us,
vision makes light of contradiction:
Granite is grass in the holy meadow of the soul's repose.

Like many of Hall's poems, the poems of *The Happy Man* have generational and regenerational impulses; one must live both through and beyond those generational echoes and reverberations. The spirits and souls and characters here have chosen to stand, as steadfastly as they are able, against the wastes of time. These poems want to insist upon a transcendence (though Hall would prefer, of course, Eckhart's "repose" as the term to embody that transcendence) over the body's destruction and the world's griefs. There is a determined, at times willed, quality to this insistence—I don't mean *forced*, I mean *chosen*—that makes me feel that though Hall sees the spirit's victory as natural, perhaps as natural as the body's betrayal and the occasional vacuum of human values, he still sees and wishes to honor the fierce courage of his characters, the courage necessary to find belief or, rather, repose. In this way, confronting the seeming "defeat" of mortality, the spirit joins itself to the timelessness of landscape and natural process. To be *of* nature is, in a basic way, to be no longer the *object* of its seemingly destructive (through regenerative) processes. Merging times and generations, Hall concludes *The Happy Man* with a gesture of affirmation and generosity and triumph; it is a simple offering, as simple as the milk his grandfather carries, or the words he holds forth:

From the Studebaker's backseat, on our Sunday drives,
I watched her earrings sway. Then I walked uphill
beside an old man carrying buckets
under birches on an August day. Striding at noontime,
I looked at wheat and at river cities. In the crib

my daughter sighed opening her eyes. I kissed the cheek
of my father dying. By the pond an acorn fell.
You listening here, you reading these words as I write them,
I offer this cup to you: Though we drink
from this cup every day, we will never drink it dry.

HIDING THE ROPE

Eric Torgersen

The Happy Man, 1986

"Ah," I thought, the first time I heard the title of Donald Hall's new book of poems, *The Happy Man*: "Roethke." Theodore Roethke's manic villanelle of the same title says, "The right thing happens to the happy man." But no, it's Tolstoy, and it's not so cheerful: "Behold me then, a man happy and in good health, hiding the rope in order not to hang myself to the rafters of the room where every night I went to sleep alone; behold me no longer shooting, lest I should yield to the too easy temptation . . ." "Merle Bascom's .22" is the book's most frightening expression of this mysterious, absolute, seemingly a-psychological rebellion against living, rising out of what sounds like it ought to be a source of happiness:

> One day I was walking
> alone and imagined a granddaughter visiting:
> She loved the old place; she swam in the summer pond
>   with us;
> she walked with us in red October; she grew older, she fell
> in love with a neighbor, she married. . . . As I daydreamed,
> suddenly I was seized by a fit of revulsion:
> I thought: 'Must I go through all that again? Must I live
> another twenty years?'

The poem ends with the speaker going to an old friend, asking him to hide the firing pin of an old .22, once his father's, which he now fears will tempt him one day. The end of the poem is devastating: "I cannot throw it away; it was my father's gift." The inheritance, then, includes not only the gun but the impulse to turn it on himself.

But the book's pitiless vision is tempered by a ground-note of continuity, a knowledge and acceptance of the passing of time, seasons, generations. In 1975 Hall left his teaching position at the University of Michigan, and moved to the family farm in New Hampshire where he had spent summers as a boy, there to support himself by his writing. Though Eagle Pond Farm has already entered the subject matter of the previous book, *Kicking the Leaves*, in *The Happy Man* it has gone all the way in, informing the book in sound, image, story, time-sense, vision. Necessarily, since it is a farm, and has been in the family over generations, the vision it informs does not fail to encompass death. Of course it did not give birth to the foolishly happy book one might have imagined, in which the happy man retired to the old home-place grows grandfatherly and satisfied and wise because he has made the right choices.

In *The Happy Man*, the vision of continuity is most present in "Twelve Seasons," a poem in twelve twelve-line stanzas that takes the reader through the months, focusing not on any one person's life but on the shared life of a community. Another source of this poem's strength, and the book's strength underlying its bleak moments, is Hall's wonderfully full-throated use of American English, without eccentricity or bombast, as in this winter stanza about making a boiled dinner:

Hook a six-pound slab of pale brisket from the barrel's
brine. Bring it to a boil in a great kettle
and pour off the flaky water. Boil it again
four hours and a half. Spiral the peel
from a dense yellow turnip and cleaver it
into eight wedges; drop in the pot for the last
hour's boiling. Ten minutes later put the potatoes in,
scrubbed in their jackets. With half an hour left,
add carrots and the Turkish domes of onions.
For the last twelve minutes lay chunks of cabbage,
green-white and quavering, on the erupting surface
of the inexhaustible pot over the assembling fire.

At the center of the book is the largest poem, "Shrubs Burnt
Away," which, a note tells us, is to be followed by two more
sections to form a long poem called *Build a House*. It has what
must be the most deadly one-two combination of epigraphs in
recent literature. In the first of them, Matthew Arnold asks
rhetorically which situations do not lend themselves to poetry,
and answers himself this way: "They are those in which the
suffering finds no vent in action; in which a continuous state
of mental distress is prolonged, unrelieved by incident, hope
or resistance; in which there is everything to be endured, nothing
to be done." It is as if Hall's poem is an answer to Arnold's
implicit challenge to make a poem out of this intractable un-
poetic state. Here is the second epigraph, to which the name
Hsu Hsia-k'o is attached: "Mi-t'o Temple after thirty li. A most
desolate spot . . . For fear of them hiding tigers, all trees and
shrubs have been burnt." This gives the poem its title and central metaphor.

The poem opens with the memory of a story told by a mother
to a small boy and his sister:

> Once a little boy and his sister — my mother lay
> on top of the quilt, narrow and tense, whispering —
> found boards piled up, deep in the woods, and nails,
> and built a house for themselves, and nobody knew
> that they built their house each day in the woods. . . .

The boy, now a man, returns to the memory and transforms it:

> As I sit by myself, middle-aged in my yellow chair,
> staring at the vacant book of the ceiling, starting
> the night's bottle, aureoled with cigarette smoke
> in the unstoried room, I daydream to build
> the house of dying. . . .

The poem ranges widely over time and place, but returns always to the pitiless vision of the middle-aged man in the yellow chair, staring, drinking, daydreaming, his gaze burning away every shrub that might still conceal danger. What he finds as his mind ranges is counterpointed by a female voice, a sister voice (whatever its literal identity) that tells its own pained stories and frightening dreams. The poem itself is highly composed, full of patterns of recurrence, but I sense that some parts of its architecture will not be clear until it is published whole, at which time *Build a House* promises to be among the major long poems of Hall's large and accomplished generation.

The counterpoint of male and female is important in *The Happy Man*: the final two sections are called "Men Driving Cars" — it is here that Merle Bascom faces his father's gun — and "Sisters." The poems in "Sisters," taken as a whole, are the most redemptive in the book. "For an Exchange of Rings" holds up delicately yet intimately the moment of Keats's engagement to Fanny Brawne, preserving it even though the wedding was never to come and Keats had only a short time to live. "The Impossible Marriage" imagines, good-naturedly, the inconceivable union of Walt Whitman and Emily Dickinson. "Acorns" and "Granite and Grass" figure the relation of male and female by subtle metaphors. The final poem, "The Day I Was Older," written of the day on which Hall's age surpassed the age of his father when he died, ends this way: "You listening here, you reading these words as I write them, / I offer this cup to you: Though we drink / from this cup every day, we will never drink it dry."

THEIR CRAFT OR SULLEN ART

❧   David Lehman   ☙

The One Day, 1988

It took Donald Hall 17 years to write *The One Day* (Ticknor & Fields, $16.95, $8.95 paper), which is Whitmanic in a more orthodox sense [than James Schuyler's long poems]: loud, sweeping, multitudinous, an act of the imperial imagination. A sustained and unified work in three parts rather than a conventional collection, it is the poet's present to himself for his 60th birthday in September. I have no hesitation in declaring it a major book — its passion and urgency are rare and remarkable. Basketball players have a word for hot shooting: the man with the hot hand is shooting "unconscious." This seems an apt description of Hall's method and his magic in *The One Day*.

Hall tells us he began writing *The One Day* in fits and bursts, very rapidly, not knowing where he was going; he reports that "it seemed like dictation" at first, like "signals from other lives." Only gradually did he shape the work into a sequence consisting of "ten-line bricks" (stanzas) used to construct a metaphoric house. In the first and third sections of the book, a male voice and female one (in Roman and italic type, respectively) do the talking. We begin in crisis: "unfit / to work or love, aureoled with cigarette smoke / in the unstoried room, I daydream to build / the house of dying." We end with an assertion of order. This is the poem's climactic line: "Work, love, build a house, and die. But build a house."

The "Four Classic Texts" that form the book's purgatorial middle seciton are magnificent, particularly "Prophecy," with its rejections and threats ("and the earth [will] split open like a corpse's gassy / stomach and the sun turn as black as a widow's skirt") and "History," with its violent montage of historical episodes. High on Hall's thematic agenda are age and aging, rage and raging against the dying of the light, but his powerful rhetorical gestures and dazzling juxtapositions communicate a pleasure even beyond the skillful treatment of such themes.

AN ENLARGING PLEASURE

❦ Stephen Sandy ❧

The One Day, 1988

Donald Hall has written a long poem. Quite possibly *The One Day* is the major accomplishment of his career. Hall's poem is serious, ambitious, graceful. *The One Day* has the force of gravity which a long poem gains in the ear's mind, and an impressive density; a tensile strength resulting from a quilt of narrative shot through with meditation; a startling rhetoric of denunciation; and a judgmental stance which shows Hall at the noontide of his thoughtful powers.

The One Day is a splendid accomplishment, and a demanding one. Great craft informs this poem, the sort of employment of techniques and devices one scarcely hopes to find in anyone's work anymore. It's as if he's rolled all the Silver Ghosts out of their garages, and we find them well tuned and running, gleaming in the sun, outdoing the rusted Toyotas of our penny-ante poetry. Reading *The One Day* is like experiencing a fast run, with appropriate stops, through the modes, techniques, and manners of Western poetry, from Old Testament invective or Psalmic praise to Theocritan pastoral romance, to Romantic narrative. The presence of Juvenal, Virgil, Dryden, Frost,

Whitman, Ginsberg, and Geoffrey Hill as tutelary spirits is detectable; and a feast of echos and allusions awaits those invited to it by their familiarity with salient poetic texts.

Made up of 110 ten-line stanzas, *The One Day* is the narrative of a life related alternately by an "I" (who, as Hall says in a postscript, "will be taken as the author") and by a woman sculptor, who suffers many travails and, finally, is summoned to The White House to receive a medal. Other voices blend to make a choral consciousness (Hall quotes Picasso, "Every human being is a colony"), but the male and female narrators constitute the poet's persona which, so to speak, has undergone mitotic cleavage.

The explosion — with its attendant themes of art holding out against chaos; work holding out against exhaustion; the stigmatizing of a corrupt America — is bisected by an interlude of four movements, "Prophecy," "Pastoral," "History," "Eclogue," each of which joins the indictment afresh, surveying with scorn and wit the decay, apathy, and destructive fatalism of contemporary America.

This central part, each section in a different mode, may be the most compelling piece of the poem. Here there's space only to quote from the first of the "Four Classic Texts," "Prophecy," endearing for the shimmering vibrancy of its Biblical rhetoric. From a viewpoint of privileged awareness, Hall's jeremiad employs techniques of anaphora and cataloguing, denouncing an America whose culture is exhausted and dying:

> I reject Japanese smoked oysters, potted chrysanthemums allowed to die, Tupperware parties, Ronald McDonald, Kaposi's sarcoma, the Taj Mahal, Holsteins wearing electronic necklaces, the Algonquin, Tunisian aqueducts,

> Phi Beta Kappa keys, the Hyatt Embarcadero, carpenters
> jogging on the median . . .

The voice is empowered to judge and to punish:

> I will strike from the hill with rainclouds of lava;
> I will strike from darkened air
> with melanoma in the shape of decorative hexagonals.

The tone is briskly serious, convincing; Hall unabashedly
engages Old Testament prophecy, even invoking Yahweh: "When
priests and policemen / strike my body's match, Jehovah will
flame out; / Jehovah will suck air from the vents of bombshelters." Rage flourishes (the luminous closure of "Prophecy"
is a memorable passage of apocalyptic writing) and is made strong
and clean-cutting by an awareness of human failure (exemplified
by his own, as the narrator tells us elsewhere in this long text)
and by a righteousness made credible by articulate utterance.
Condemnation is strengthened as well for being balanced by
the theme of the final part, which prescribes while it celebrates
a wise prudence in our relations with the earth, its creatures,
our desires. "I marry the creation that stays / in place to be
worked at, day after day."

The difficulties of writing a long poem are many. Complexities
of organization grow at a geometric rather than an arithmetic rate,
for one. For another there is the inkling we now have that since
few read poetry (and die every day, as Williams said, for want of
what is found there) and since the few who do are hipped on
tidy, affordable studio poems whose authors give quarter for
stretching mind or spirit, there's little hope that more than a hand-
ful of aficionados will read a long poetic text from opening strophe
to closing lines. Stevens remarked that, "anyone who has read
a long poem . . . knows how the poem comes to possess the reader

and how it naturalizes him in its own imagination and liberates him there." For those who are up to it, reading Hall's poem will be an enlarging pleasure, and a reminder of how immediate, concrete, and pertinent to our situation a poem can be.

It is a commonplace that a serious poet aspires to write a long poem. Donald Hall's *The One Day* is ambitious in the best sense; it gives us agency, force, intelligence; it is alive with form and figure; it has (in the final part especially) a passional yet thoughtful tone that requires our assent to the whole work. Hall has said that "There is no way to be good except by trying to be great." He has embraced the need the strong poet has to write a long poem and has succeeded impressively. Hall is more than a good poet.

BIBLIOGRAPHY

Publications by Donald Hall:

BOOKS OF POETRY

To the Loud Wind and Other Poems. Pegasus Publication Series, Vol. 1, No. 1, *The Harvard Advocate*, 1955.

Exiles and Marriages. (Lamont Poetry Selection, 1955), Viking Press, New York, 1955.

The Dark Houses. Viking, 1958.

A Roof of Tiger Lilies. Viking and Andre Deutsch, London, 1963.

The Alligator Bride: Poems New and Selected. Harper & Row, New York, 1969.

The Yellow Room: Love Poems. Harper & Row, 1971.

The Town of Hill. David R. Godine, Boston, 1975.

Kicking the Leaves. Harper & Row and Secker & Warburg, London, 1978.

The Happy Man. Random House, New York, and Secker & Warburg, 1986.

The Bone Ring. (a play in verse) Story Line Press, Santa Cruz, 1987.

The One Day. (a poem in three parts) Ticknor & Fields, New York, 1988.

String Too Short to Be Saved. Viking Press, 1961. Reprinted, Godine, Boston, 1979.

Henry Moore. Harper & Row and Gollancz, London, 1966

As the Eye Moves . . . (photographs by David Finn, text by Donald Hall.) Abrams, New York, 1970.

The Pleasures of Poetry. Harper & Row, 1971.

Writing Well. Little, Brown, Boston, 1973, 1976, 1979, 1982, 1985, 1988.

Playing Around. (Co-author) Little, Brown, 1974.

Dock Ellis in the Country of Baseball. Coward McCann. New York, 1976.

Goatfoot Milktongue Twinbird. University of Michigan Press, Ann Arbor, 1978.

Remembering Poets. Harper & Row, 1978.

To Keep Moving. Hobart & William Smith Colleges Press, 1980.

The Oxford Book of American Literary Anecdotes. Oxford University Press, 1981.

The Weather for Poetry. University of Michigan Press, 1982.

Fathers Playing Catch with Sons. North Point Press, San Francisco, 1985.

The Ideal Bakery. (short stories) North Point Press, 1987.

Seasons at Eagle Pond. (essays) Ticknor & Fields, 1987.

Poetry and Ambition, University of Michigan Press, 1988.

New Poems of England and America. (with R. Pack and
L. Simpson), Meridian Books, New York, 1957.

The Poetry Sampler. Franklin Watts. 1961.

New Poets of England and America. (Second Selection)
(with R. Pack), Meridian Books, 1962.

Contemporary American Poetry. Penguin Books, London
and Baltimore, 1962. Second edition, 1972.

*A Concise Encyclopedia of English and American Poetry
and Poets* (with Stephen Spender), Hawthorne Books,
New York, 1963.

Poetry in English. (with Warren Taylor), Macmillan,
New York, 1963.

The Faber Book of Modern Verse (New Edition with
Supplement). Faber, London. 1965.

The Modern Stylists. The Free Press, New York, 1968.

A Choice of Whitman's Verse. Faber and Faber. 1968.

Man and Boy. Franklin Watts, 1968.

A Writer's Reader. (with D. Emblen) Little, Brown,
Boston, 1976, 1979, 1982, 1985, 1988.

Claims for Poetry. University of Michigan Press, 1982.

To Read Literature. Holt, 1980, 1983, 1986.

To Read Poetry. Holt, 1981.

To Read Fiction. Holt, 1987.

The Contemporary Essay. Bedford Books, 1984, 1989.

Oxford Book of Children's Verse in America. Oxford
University Press, 1985.

Andrew the Lion Farmer. Franklin Watts, New York, 1959.

Riddle Rat. Frederick Warne, New York, 1977.

Ox Cart Man. The Viking Press, New York, 1979. (Caldecott, 1980.)

The Man Who Lived Alone. David Godine, 1984.

THE EDITOR

Liam Rector was born in 1949. His first book of poems, *The Sorrow of Architecture*, was published in 1984, and he has received Guggenheim and National Endowment for the Arts fellowships for his poetry. He has worked administering literary programs at the Academy of American Poets, the Folger Shakespeare Library, the Literature Program at the National Endowment for the Arts, and Associated Writing Programs, where he is currently the executive director. He has taught at George Mason University, Goucher College, the Phillips Academy at Andover, and currently lives in the Tidewater region of Virginia with his wife Mary and daughter Virginia.